TWELVE SCHOOLS THAT SUCCEED

By
Mary Ann Horenstein

Phi Delta Kappa Educational Foundation
Bloomington, Indiana

Cover design by
Victoria Voelker

Library of Congress Catalog Number 93-86008
ISBN 0-87367-462-6

To my husband, Don, who offers me
boundless emotional and editorial support and love.

Table of Contents

Introduction

Imagine a school so exciting that parents move 2,000 miles so that their children can attend it. What about a school in which, when a student announces that he spent only an hour and a half on homework last night, his classmates warn him to work harder?

These scenarios seem far-fetched, but they are true in schools that succeed. I wanted to find out why.

My quest to discover why some schools succeed took me to 12 Blue Ribbon schools. These highly successful schools are a few of the many Blue Ribbon secondary schools chosen during the 1991 federal recognition program. They are schools where learning is valued, teachers and students work closely to attain mutually determined goals, parents are involved with their children's education, and student success is the norm.

All across the United States, thinking people are concerned about the state of secondary education. Our world has changed. The traditional social structures of family, church, and neighborhood have been transformed. In some places crime rates have skyrocketed, powered by increased drug abuse. Unemployment, poverty, and homelessness can be found in every state. These problems cannot be blamed on the schools, but it is important to examine critically the schools' responses to the crises of society.

Unfortunately, a look inside many schools might lead one to believe that time has stood still. Students continue to be placed in the same graded classes and taught the same subject matter by the same teaching techniques. Many students continue to learn 19th-century answers to 20th-century questions. Societal changes challenge schools to accept new responsibilities. The pressures mount for schools to meet the demands of a changing world and to fulfill mandates to educate youth about high-risk topics, such as sex, drugs, and AIDS. Yet the school day is no longer and no different today than it was a decade ago.

Educators and politicians may argue about the shape of the ideal school, but outstanding schools already exist. The 12 schools in this book are alive and healthy; they are exemplars that can set attainable standards for the nation.

The Blue Ribbon schools are selected annually by the United States Department of Education. Schools from throughout the United States enter the competition each year, with secondary schools and elementary schools being chosen in alternate years. Becoming a Blue Ribbon school is a complex and lengthy process. Any school in the United States may submit an application to its state department of education. The selection criteria include leadership, curriculum and instruction, and organizational vitality, plus such objective indicators of success as measures of student achievement and daily student and teacher attendance rates.

The individual states select the best applications and forward them to the federal Department of Education. After further winnowing by a review panel of educators, elected officials, representatives of the education press, parents, and business representatives, the Department of Education sends two site visitors to each of the remaining contenders to confirm that they are indeed achieving what they claim. Those schools that survive this final step become Blue Ribbon schools.

The Blue Ribbon program was designed to stimulate school improvement. Each participating school is required to conduct a self-evaluation. The principals of schools previously recognized by the program often are linked with those of potential candidates, and the candidate schools collaborate with national organizations. In addition, the recognition provided to the pursuit of excellence stimulates school improvement.

These schools are not theoretical models; they are functioning institutions that are succeeding now. They are far from perfect; in fact, they all contend with serious problems. Yet they are oases of learning. Many of their programs may be modified for use in other school districts.

The 12 Blue Ribbon secondary schools described in this book represent a cross-section of America. They are found in large cities, suburbs, small towns, and rural areas across the country and in both wealthy and poor communities. In some cases the student body is nearly all white; in others almost all African-American; in one case predominantly Asian. Several have a mixture of ethnic groups. However, while these schools are all very different, they do have many things in common.

Most of these schools have a vision. They have clear goals, and administration and faculty work together to meet those goals. Some post their goals in the school to remind faculty and students of where they are heading. They have strong administrators who keep those goals in mind when they hire and evaluate teachers.

The teachers in these schools are empowered. They know that their voices count, whether dealing with students or initiating curriculum changes. But the teachers pay a price for that empowerment: They work harder than most teachers in other schools. The kids feel empowered, too. They have both formal and informal ways of making themselves heard: a strong student council, a principal who keeps his or her office door open, a special faculty member whose job it is to listen to their concerns.

Each of these schools has created an atmosphere where it is "cool" to be smart and to learn. Many of the students have discovered that success in school is one way to improve their lives. Each of the schools starts with the belief that students can learn and want to learn. When a student is having trouble, the school offers a strong support system.

While classroom learning is prized at these schools, the arts, athletics, and other kinds of experiences also have great value. The schools have dance programs, theater programs, and many valued clubs. Scholarly learning is seen as only one kind of growth. Who would expect in a school of 1,000 students that there would be enough interest in dance to fill classes every period of the day? And what about a school with three bands, three orchestras, three other instrumental ensembles, and six choruses?

These are schools whose walls are coming down — between the disciplines, between faculty and parents, between students and teachers, and between the school and the community. They break the traditional mold of teenagers confined to experiences within the school building and teachers isolated in their classrooms. These are schools in which teachers observe each other and take part in team teaching. These are schools in which students may spend part of their day in a community business or with a mentor, work with a group of elementary school youngsters, visit the elderly at a nursing home, conduct on-site research, or take a course at a local college.

These Blue Ribbon schools have taken on the unmet challenges of our changed society. They provide a strong support system for students. They focus on teaching job skills that their graduates will need for a bright future. They connect their students with the community beyond the classroom door. In short, they supplement the diminishing influence of family, neighborhood, and church in order to offer their students a life experience, not just a school experience.

These schools face different educational challenges, and they meet them in a variety of ways. Educators and parents should consider these schools as models that they can adapt to the needs of their own districts. The telephone number of each school is provided so that interested readers can call to learn more about how to enhance the learning experiences of students in their own communities.

Old Orchard Beach High School

Old Orchard Beach High School is located on T-for-Turn Road, Old Orchard Beach, Maine 04064. Telephone: (207) 934-4461. The principal is Dr. Grace Cantara.

Old Orchard Beach, Maine, is not a community where you would expect to find an outstanding high school. In the summer it is a honky tonk beach town with motorcycle racers, bars, pizza joints, a population of more than 120,000 — and miles of beautiful coastline. In the winter the tourist attractions close up, and the town shrinks to about 6,500 residents, mostly blue-collar workers with modest educational backgrounds.

The high school has a student population of 290, with 47 special education students. It wasn't even accredited until 1984. But it has become an astonishing center of learning with a professional staff that makes a difference in the lives of its students. While only about 20% of the parents in Old Orchard Beach attended college, the school sends 65% of its graduates to some form of post-secondary education. Indeed, many of the graduates are the first in their family to complete high school. Some go off to Ivy League colleges.

Block Scheduling

The outstanding professional staff of Old Orchard Beach High School, under the leadership of their young and exuberant principal, Dr. Grace Cantara, clearly are doing a lot of things right. For one thing, they take risks. Dissatisfied with the daily schedule of seven 45-minute classes, the faculty decided on block scheduling to restructure the school day. This represented a major change.

Several faculty members visited a school that had block scheduling. They were impressed with what they saw but frightened by the

5

enormity of the impact it would have on their school. As a faculty committed to the idea of decision by consensus, they wrestled long and hard over the issue. Finally, the change to block scheduling won out. After preparing during the spring and summer, they initiated the new schedule when school opened in September 1992.

At Old Orchard Beach, block scheduling caused a major overhaul in the school day. The old 10-minute homeroom was eliminated, and students began school 20 minutes earlier than before. These changes have added 30 minutes to each day. Most classes now meet for 80 minutes. Science and math, with labs, meet for 120 minutes. There are four periods each day, giving students eight classes that meet every other day. A few 40-minute classes are clustered around the 40-minute lunch break. Special events, such as visits by college representatives, also occur during lunch periods.

Consultants initially helped teachers plan for the longer classes, but the faculty quickly adapted to the new format. Several positive results were immediately obvious. For example, science classes gained valuable time for labs and hands-on experiences. Other teachers have initiated cooperative learning, discussion groups, and film viewing — with time to finish activities during a single period. Portfolio assessment has become easier to accomplish. Physical education teachers can complete an activity and still give students enough time to change before their next class. Perhaps most significant, since classes now meet every other day, students have two days to process classroom events and complete homework. They have time to think about that social studies discussion or to write that English paper.

Problems of Democracy

Old Orchard Beach teachers demand a great deal of critical thinking from their students. This demand is evident in many courses but nowhere more than in Problems of Democracy, a course especially important for seniors who do not plan to go to college. The course teaches the complexities of citizenship in a democratic society, beginning with a study of United States history from 1945 to the present. Students analyze issues from each presidential administration, with emphasis on the present. For example, on my visit to a classroom right after the second Rodney King trial, I found a heated discussion under way based on a national news magazine's assessment of the verdict. Questions were fast and difficult. Whose advocate is the press in the article? How might politicians in this area best handle criticism? Could the Rodney King drama happen here in Old Orchard Beach? Whose side are the police on? What can you say about a country where a jury behaves as the Los Angeles jury did? There were no right answers; many responses were sought to each question. The room was alive with thoughtful excitement.

Since this course prepares students for citizenship, students tackle many topics. For example, an AIDS curriculum, developed by the Family Planning Association, is taught here. Students join in small-group discussions with faculty leaders, including the principal, and focus on how decisions are made that affect their lives, such as preventing AIDS.

Recently, a new dimension was added to the Problems of Democracy class: mandatory community service. Teacher Michael Angelosante says, "I want students to realize that the community only works if we give to it." Students have volunteered in the police and fire departments, the local elementary school, the township clerk's office, and other local non-profit organizations. During the first year, students were required to give only five hours, although many contributed more. The requirement will be raised for future years.

Other courses are similarly demanding. Geometry, for instance, is taught through problem solving but also is treated as an art; the walls are filled with geometric artwork. In science classes textbooks are used mainly as references, and teachers create their own labs.

In a biology class discussion about determining the age of a tree, one student responded to the question by saying, "It says in the book . . ." "Don't tell me what it says in the book or you'll never learn to think," interrupted the teacher.

A world cultures class is interdisciplinary, created by combining a class in Western civilization and sophomore English. Block scheduling facilitates such classes, allowing team teaching and double-size student groups to work together. The research in this course is demanding, and some students arrive at the school at 6:30 a.m. for help with their papers before classes begin. The class recently went out to the football field and made a timeline of the history of the Earth, in the process discovering that Western history took up only six inches of the one hundred yards.

Programs for Special Students

More than 16% of the student body are special education students. For many of these youngsters and for students at risk of school failure, several hands-on programs offer specialized opportunities to learn and plan for the future. One of the most exciting ventures is a picture-frame shop, a hands-on experience to teach students how to build and run a business. Students learn all the skills for framing: how to make moldings, cut mats and glass, dry mount, and laminate. When I visited the school, the students had created a showroom next to the shop and were getting ready to take orders from school district employees, thus learning such business procedures as keeping inventories and preparing bills.

As sales begin, profits will be returned to the shop. Starting the business is a slow procedure, since the students themselves do most of the planning and make the decisions. Planning and running the business is an important learning experience that gives students skills they can use in their own future jobs.

Another hands-on course for at-risk students is called Space Simulation Technology. Students work all year in small teams building a space vehicle, designing a space station (called *Habitat*) on the school's athletic field, and establishing a mission control center inside the school to keep in touch with the "astronauts." A recent spaceship was made from an old car that the school bought for $100. For *Habitat* the students were required to plan food and equipment for the astronauts. A local business even donated a chemical toilet.

In late May, the school, the press, and the entire community turned out for the launch. The teenage astronauts took off in their capsule to the space station. During three days "in space," the students worked with teachers both at the *Habitat* and in mission control. The simulation taught them a great deal about space flight and gave them practical experience about living in a hostile environment. In addition, it was one of the most exciting adventures in the teenagers' lives.

The school reaches out to at-risk students in other ways as well. Project HELP, a group of teachers and community service providers, meets weekly to discuss students who have special needs. Every meeting ends with a strategy to help the students in question. Most at-risk students are encouraged to join a support group, and there are many kinds of groups, focusing on topics that range from better decision making to avoiding substance abuse and stopping smoking.

Nearly 40 Old Orchard Beach students have been trained as peer helpers. They have learned such techniques as effective listening, the importance of confidentiality, and how to conduct role-play activities. They are prepared to discuss difficult subjects, such as teenage pregnancy. Some of the peer helpers receive extra training in how to deal with younger children. Many volunteer as big brothers and big sisters in the local elementary school, less than a block away.

Another community outreach has been a schoolwide effort to get some former dropouts back in the school. Dropouts are contacted; and flexible, manageable schedules are arranged for those who want to continue their education.

One of the real risks in a town like Old Orchard Beach is the lure of alcohol and other drugs. During the summer, with the huge influx of transients, drugs are plentiful. Students who get hooked can be helped by a group called SAVE (Substance Abuse Volunteer Effort), which maintains a continuing substance abuse prevention plan.

Each year after senior awards night, the SAVE committee buses the entire senior class to a restaurant in Portland, approximately 15 miles away. Seniors and their parents are treated to dinner; then the parents leave, and the students and faculty have activities throughout the night, culminating in a candlelight ceremony at dawn. They are then bused safely home again to Old Orchard Beach.

In a related school effort, all sophomores (as well as seventh-graders from the district's middle school) participate in a three-day, off-campus, substance abuse awareness workshop. Without bells or the usual school distractions, they concentrate on absorbing information about drugs, talk about sexuality and self-esteem, and become a more closely knit group.

Empowerment

Most ideas for new courses come from the faculty, who know they will receive administrative support for well-planned ventures. But empowerment and administrative support are not limited to the faculty at Old Orchard Beach. The students feel empowered as well. The student council not only takes charge of pep rallies and similar events, it also involves itself in issues more important to the students. All students are encouraged to bring their concerns to the student council.

For example, the school had a rule that prohibited the wearing of shorts. Unhappy with that regulation, the student council petitioned the board of education to change it. The students were pleased that the administration, although disagreeing with their petition, offered help with the presentation. "Our teachers and administrators really listened to us," said one student council officer. Their petition was granted.

Buoyed by their success in changing the dress code, the student council recently started a more controversial petition: asking the board to make condoms available at school. The students have spent time collecting data about the experiences other schools have had in their quest for condom distribution. Before approaching the board, they will hold a public forum to seek input from students, staff, and the community. No matter what the outcome, the project is providing an important learning experience.

Sister School in France

Contact with students in another country gives small-town teenagers an opportunity to expand their horizons by learning about another culture. Old Orchard Beach has a close and interesting relationship with a sister school in Mimizan, France.

Two years after Charles Lindbergh's solo flight from the United States to France, three French pilots — Armand Loti, Réné Lefèvre, and Jean Assolant — wanted to recreate the event. They brought a plane to the United States by ocean liner and then re-assembled it so that they could fly from Old Orchard Beach (Lindbergh's last stop in the United States) to Paris. Unfortunately there was a stowaway aboard, who added unnecessary weight, thus forcing the plane to land in Spain. The pilots refueled and started for Paris, but another fuel problem forced them to abandon the flight altogether at Mimizan on the coast of southwestern France.

Sixty years later, in 1989, the towns of Old Orchard Beach and Mimizan decided to commemorate the event with a joint celebration. An American delegation visited Mimizan and a French delegation came to Old Orchard Beach. Since that time, groups of students from both towns have crossed the Atlantic each year to visit the other school. The students stay with families in the community for three weeks. Local contributions pay most of the expenses of the Old Orchard Beach students.

Exchanging views with the French students is important to the teenagers from this tiny Maine town, and they invariably discover that the two towns have much in common, in spite of the language difference.

Other Features of Excellence

Like most Blue Ribbon schools, Old Orchard Beach values the arts. Instrumental music begins in the fourth grade in the school system;

and most learning occurs in school, since no student takes private lessons. In spite of the small size of the school, there is a 40-member marching band that is good enough to have become state champions three years in a row.

The theater program, which lacks a permanent staff member, eschews the usual comedies and musicals, choosing instead to present innovative, thoughtful productions. A director is employed for three weeks each year to work with students and to stage productions. The year I visited, they presented a play about child abuse that moved both parents and students and produced positive discussions throughout the community. A previous effort, a play about AIDS, was a runner-up in the southern Maine finals.

Sports produce the same enthusiastic schoolwide response as the arts. Most students participate in at least one sport. Old Orchard Beach is the smallest school in the state to have a football team, coached by three school coaches and four volunteers. But students turn out to cheer for all the teams — girls' field hockey as well as football.

Several years ago the school instituted a rule that any student receiving an F in any subject could practice with the team but not play until receiving all passing grades. According to Jay Bartner, the former high school principal who is now district superintendent, that rule has been effective; failing students are pressured by their peers to improve their grades because the team needs them.

Old Orchard Beach High School has one Advanced Placement course, English composition. The school participated in a pilot program with Dow Jones to develop the course several years ago. Assignments include feature writing and news interviews, with which students easily identify. The student body is too small for other Advanced Placement courses, but that does not seem to matter. The students are learning, growing, and gaining acceptance into good universities. Old Orchard Beach High School has broken into the cycle of poverty and limited education in the community and is helping students to move ahead with their lives.

Parents are aware of the caring environment that the school gives their children. "I moved to Old Orchard Beach because of the schools," said one mother. "I have a special needs child and the special education teachers really help him. But my other children have also gained from the programs. The administrators and staff always have time for them and make the programs work."

St. Johnsbury Academy

St. Johnsbury Academy is located at 7 Main Street, St. Johnsbury, Vermont 05819. Telephone: (802) 748-8171. The headmaster at the time of the Blue Ribbon award was Mr. Bernier L. Mayo.

St. Johnsbury Academy is a school that brings together very disparate worlds. It is both public and private, small town and cosmopolitan. It offers one of the largest selections of Advanced Placement courses in Vermont and one of the most extensive vocational programs.

St. Johnsbury was founded in 1842 as an independent academy. The academy recruits boarding students from around the world, as well as across the United States. Boarders come from Japan, Hong Kong, Korea, Bermuda, the Bahamas, and several European countries.

In the 1960s state requirements forced many small academies out of business, but St. Johnsbury survived. Currently many towns in Vermont are without a high school. Students from those towns receive a voucher to attend a school of their choice. Since the town of St. Johnsbury, like many surrounding towns, has no public high school, the academy's 136 boarding students are joined by more than 700 public day students.

St. Johnsbury Academy differs from public schools in one basic way: it is market driven. "Meeting the needs of the community isn't altruistic — it's good business," says Headmaster Bernier Mayo. "Our product is education. We have to produce what the students need, at a price the community can afford." The result for the town is a local school that both trains their children for vocations and prepares them for the rigors of the nation's top universities.

Interactive TV

Imagine the following problem: An excellent school is filled to capacity. There is no room for the total student population to expand, but a few empty seats remain in such small classes as Japanese and Advanced Placement Literature. Schools in nearby towns are unable to provide these courses and would like to send their students to this school, but there is no room for them except in a few classes. St. Johnsbury Academy found a creative solution to this problem without launching a building program.

The solution was interactive television. St. Johnsbury installed its system in several classrooms; and matching equipment was placed in Blue Mountain, a school 20 miles away. During 1993-94, 27 Blue Mountain students registered for three courses taught at St. Johnsbury that are not offered at their school: Anatomy and Physiology, Japanese, and Spanish. The teacher at St. Johnsbury faces several students on site and works with several other students at Blue Mountain using the video link. They all can see and talk to each other. The camera can zoom in on any student or the teacher.

A fax machine in each classroom allows for paper exchanges. When the St. Johnsbury teacher gives a test, she can observe students in both classrooms. And when the test has been completed, she watches while the Blue Mountain students send their test papers through the fax machine.

Besides offering a solution to a curriculum problem for both schools, the use of interactive television offers a hidden advantage: Students from St. Johnsbury are learning to operate the television station.

This connection with the classrooms of Blue Mountain is only the beginning of a new relationship among Vermont schools. Within a few years, the electronic classrooms probably will be in three or four other schools. At the other end of the spectrum, Dartmouth College, an hour's drive from St. Johnsbury in Hanover, New Hampshire, is developing new applications for interactive television with four secondary schools, including St. Johnsbury, and one museum. Transmissions of lectures at Dartmouth or a combination of live video and film clips may be part of future classes at the school. For example, a doctor might appear on television to explain a patient's clogged arteries while viewers simultaneously view an actual picture of the patient's heart.

"Education grew out of a medieval model, with people coming to a university to learn," explains St. Johnsbury Headmaster Mayo. "Now we still need the knowledge, but we don't have to travel. The resources can emanate from the university to the greater community."

St. Johnsbury has a strong commitment to the community. A field house built several years ago reserves space in its pool, weight room, and athletic courts for the community first and intramural activities second. The school's theater is open for community use. On most weekdays, classrooms are available after 2:30 p.m. to local groups, as well as to a community college. This kind of sharing draws the school and the town together.

Vocational Curriculum

The academy must meet many needs, given its diverse population. Its vocational curriculum is one of its greatest achievements. Many courses combine science and technology; and learning tends to be "event-driven," rather than structured around content.

The U.S. Department of Energy sponsors an annual competition in which students, mostly college engineering students, build electric cars and race them 250 miles. The winner is determined as much by endurance and safety as by speed. When St. Johnsbury heard about the competition two years ago, the faculty and students decided to enter. The academy offers courses in auto mechanics, technology, electricity, and physics, so students had the basic knowledge for such a project. They found an old wreck and completely rebuilt it as an electric car. When the day of the race came, the young drivers of St. Johnsbury drove to victory past the college students, including those from the Massachusetts Institute of Technology. (A year later MIT edged them out of first place, but St. Johnsbury finished a close second.)

The electric car provided a double victory. Students in the St. Johnsbury video training program captured the race on tape and later won first prize in a video contest.

Students learn building trades following the same kind of event-driven curriculum. Every year they build a house, from laying out the lot and drawing the blueprints to constructing the actual building. Recently the students entered a contest to build a super energy-efficient house. The goal is to create a local house in which the total annual energy bill will be $500. St. Johnsbury's weather is very cold, but the academy already has calculated that the energy bill for their house will be $350. St. Johnsbury Academy may be the only school to enter the contest; most of the contestants are professional builders, insulators, and electrical contractors.

Students in this project are experimenting with new, efficient building techniques. When they poured the foundation, they used styrofoam forms, instead of wood, for extra insulation. A 240-foot thermal well with a heat pump provides heat in the winter and cools the house in the summer. They are experimenting with a microwave clothes dryer. Regardless of whether they win the contest, these students are becoming highly qualified for the building trades.

Both of these projects cut across the curriculum. An understanding of physics is essential in order to design the heating system for the house. Measuring and cutting the lumber rely heavily on math skills. And in order to communicate with others about their project, the students need the skills learned in their English classes.

The faculty of St. Johnsbury try to be sensitive to the vocational needs of the community. They recently instituted courses in diesel mechanics and tractor-trailer driving because those skills lead to jobs in the St. Johnsbury area. The school's electricity shop is so sophisticated that students receive apprenticeship credit for their class work. St. Johnsbury's vocational program is not just for high school students; it's also a regional vocational center. It is not unusual to see 10 students working with a teacher on a project in the electricity shop while two adults are studying independently.

St. Johnsbury also schedules an array of Advanced Placement courses in language and literature, physics, chemistry, calculus, computer science, and American and world history. The school has the widest selection of Advanced Placement courses in Vermont. Although vocational and Advanced Placement courses often are characterized as opposite ends of the curricular spectrum, students move freely among all the courses. An academically gifted student may take drafting or electronics. A vocational student might be in Advanced Placement science or math courses. Classes are homogeneously grouped according to ability, but it is understood that students' abilities vary among disciplines.

A Tradition of Support

St. Johnsbury exemplifies a tradition of putting students first. For example, sports are an important part of the academy. A wide range of interscholastic and intramural teams can be found on campus. Sometimes teams are maintained because they contribute to students' development, in spite of limited interest. During the year preceding my visit, only a few girls went out for field hockey. The administration considered dropping the team; but when they watched a practice one day, they saw several girls on the team who were not involved in any other sports activities. They kept the team.

This attitude of support extends to all areas. At the beginning of every year, all students are given a form in their English classes, asking if they would like to join a support group. Some groups are devoted to specific problems, such as drug abuse or sexual abuse. Others are more general, consisting of students who just need to talk. Various groups are led by counselors, the psychologist, the nurse, and some teachers. They meet weekly at lunch time; nobody outside the group knows about a student's participation. These groups become an important part of each student's life. Last year more than 100 teenagers participated in these groups.

Helping its many foreign students fit in at the academy is another complex process. Several years of classroom instruction in English are mandatory for acceptance at St. Johnsbury, but some students arrive having received little conversational instruction. New students whose English is marginal spend six weeks before school opens taking conversation classes and living with a local family in order to improve their communication skills. These students often form close relationships with their host families and return to visit them during vacations.

When school opens, these students usually are placed in English-as-a-second-language (ESL) classes for part of their instructional day. Some students spend the whole day in ESL; their goal is to become proficient enough to move into all regular classes. A Japanese-speaking teacher, also a resident in one of the dormitories, is an important role model and advisor for many of the Asian students, most of whom plan to study at an American university after they graduate from St. Johnsbury.

Regular English-speaking students also are offered academic support. Students with learning deficiencies are placed in a study-skills program every day, instead of the usual study hall. Four days a week, they receive individual tutoring; one day a week, there is an organized presentation on a specific skill, such as taking notes.

To prepare students for the St. Johnsbury experience, guidance counselors visit the middle schools of incoming ninth-graders to learn which new students may be precarious learners. Students who need help in a subject area are paired with peer tutors who have strengths in that area. About 50 pairs of students usually are involved in the tutoring program.

Last year the school created a "Lazarus Program" for students whose behavior was so outrageous that their expulsion had been recommended. In this program, instead of forcing a student to leave the school, a member of the staff works with him or her full time for several weeks. The staff member's goal is to understand the student's behavior and to help the student deal appropriately with the problem. To date, of the four students placed in the Lazarus Program, two have been successfully returned to regular classes, one has left the school, and one is still being counseled.

The tradition of support at St. Johnsbury Academy also extends to teachers. Working conditions are excellent; faculty seldom leave the school to work elsewhere. If the administration knows a year in advance that there will be an opening, the headmaster hires a new teacher as an intern for two-fifths time during the year before the vacancy occurs. This teacher is given a small teaching load and works with a mentor to prepare for the unique challenges of St. Johnsbury. These interns also start work two weeks early in the fall in order to receive a thorough orientation, and throughout the year they participate in monthly dinner discussions with master teachers. They also take courses and attend workshops and conferences. Because St. Johnsbury is a boarding school, the interns may obtain free room and board in exchange for some duties in the dormitories.

In order to facilitate continued teacher development, St. Johnsbury mandates that all teachers earn a master's degree within eight years after being hired and continue to earn at least six graduate credits every five years after that. The school also pays for all courses.

The St. Johnsbury tradition of putting students first also extends to the professional development of school administrators. All administrators teach at least one course annually, in order to keep in close contact with the students and to stay in touch with the real heart of education — what goes on in the classroom.

Eleanor Roosevelt High School

Eleanor Roosevelt High School is located at 7601 Hanover Parkway, Greenbelt, Maryland 20770. Telephone: (301) 345-7500. The principal at the time of the Blue Ribbon award was Dr. Gerald L. Boarman.

A search for an American melting pot in microcosm need go no further than Eleanor Roosevelt High School. Located in suburban Washington, D.C., in one of three planned cities of the Roosevelt era, Eleanor Roosevelt is the largest high school in Maryland. Of the school's 2,750 students, 45% are African-American, 45% white, and 10% (and growing) Asian and Hispanic.

In socioeconomic terms, the student population is just as diverse. Students come from exceedingly wealthy neighborhoods, very poor neighborhoods, and all the gradations in between. What these students have in common is that they all desire to be at Eleanor Roosevelt.

During my visit to the school, I heard a story about a family that made an offer on a house just outside the Eleanor Roosevelt service area. Their teenager, therefore, would be required to apply for admission to the school without any guarantee of acceptance. The family wrote their real estate contract so that it would be voided if the student was not admitted to the school. The family decided that getting their child into Eleanor Roosevelt High School was more important than buying the house of their dreams.

Science and Technology Center

Eleanor Roosevelt serves as a standard comprehensive high school for 60% of its students; 40% are there because of the Science and Technology Center. One of only two in Maryland, the Science and Technology Center offers a challenging curriculum in math and science; students apply to enter the highly selective program. The center offers structured sequences of courses in science, mathematics, pre-engineering technology, and computer science, plus standard humanities and language arts courses. Eleventh- and twelfth-grade students focus on biology, physical science, or pre-engineering technology and have opportunities to enter a variety of scientific and engineering competitions. They are required to take some Advanced Placement courses, and every student must take a research practicum in which they complete a major research project.

Some of the students have a mentor outside the school, with whom they work on their projects. This outside contact gives them exposure to a professional in their field of interest and often to equipment that is not available at school. For example, Alison Ryan, one of the students I met, is interested in marine biology. She has two mentors, a professor and a graduate student at the University of Maryland. Alison's interest is coral, and in her research she is looking for the main living organism that erodes coral. Through this project, Alison learns about her mentors' work and pursues her own specific research.

Another student is doing DNA research at the National Cancer Institute. A student who wants to become an aeronautical engineer for NASA is working on micro-circuits with a mentor at Goddard Space Center, only a few minutes from the school. Several students are doing projects at the Air and Space Museum and other branches of the Smithsonian Museum.

Many students operate at a high level in science and technology, so it is not surprising that Eleanor Roosevelt offers one of the largest Advanced Placement programs in the United States. Approximately 1,000 students take at least one Advanced Placement course. More students at Eleanor Roosevelt take AP Chemistry than at any other school, and the school boasts one of the largest enrollments in AP Calculus.

Teachers encourage students to take hard courses and to set their sights high. Some ninth-grade students complete sample AP writing assignments, for instance, to discover whether they can handle Advanced Placement English classes. AP Art, in which students prepare a portfolio of original work, is a recent addition to the curriculum.

Support Services

To help every student succeed, Eleanor Roosevelt offers a variety of support services and courses. All ninth-graders take a study-skills course focusing on organizational skills, taking notes, using computers, vocabulary enrichment, and the development of self-esteem. The school's goal is to prevent problems by helping students to achieve early and lasting success. Ninth-grade discipline problems have declined and grade point averages have risen slightly since the course was implemented.

Students having academic difficulty can be tutored by members of the National Honor Society at lunch in a special section of the cafeteria. After-school tutoring is more difficult to arrange, since many students live far from the school and there are no late buses. Tutoring also is available from University of Maryland students and through Greenbelt Cares, a community volunteer organization.

For students in severe academic trouble, there is Operation SWEEP. This program targets students with a low grade point average, high absenteeism, or a perceived lack of self-esteem. Teachers recommend students for the program every fall, or students may ask to be placed in the program. Students and parents sign a contract specifying areas for improvement. The students then meet with faculty members every week or two for conferences or tutorials. They hear guest speakers and take part in incentive programs that emphasize the value of doing well academically. Once a month, students and faculty have breakfast together; and they often take out-of-school trips, such as a weekend of camping.

The SWEEP students also visit elementary schools to talk to young students who already are considered at-risk by their teachers. The teenagers often report that the younger children do not listen to them, have a short attention span, and, in fact, behave as they once did. These observations develop insights into their own behaviors.

Time Management Innovations

Teachers and administrators at Eleanor Roosevelt High School constantly seek new ways of managing time. Two innovative projects were getting under way when I visited; both involved scheduling double class periods.

Project 120 allows students to complete a year-long class in a semester by doubling the daily schedule for the class. For example, a student might cover a year of history by doubling up in the first semester and a year of English by doubling up in the second semester, rather than taking each for a full year of single classes. The double periods provide more time for discussions, debates, and labs. Many students are enthusiastic. One told me, "English is so much more fun now. We concentrate on a book, read it more quickly, and have better discussions and more time for films." The staff will gather data to evaluate Project 120 at the end of the school year.

In a related approach, students have been assigned to double periods of two courses on alternate days. This approach offers interesting team-teaching possibilities. During my visit I observed sections of chemistry and technology being taught in this way. Students are delighted with the longer labs. In addition, they are able to see relationships between the subjects that are not apparent when the subjects are taught separately. Students can move readily from theory to application. For example, in a unit on energy, the students learn the necessary chemistry involved in the making of a battery. They make their own batteries and test them. The students then use the battery's electricity to solve a problem. The students in the two classes can work with either teacher, or both groups can meet together with both teachers.

Child Development

Child Development is a sequence of classes that introduces students to the world beyond the classroom. The beginning class focuses on pre-natal and infant care. Other classes in the sequence teach parenting skills and child development. The final class explores child-oriented careers.

Practical child-care experiences are integral to these classes. Part of students' responsibilities during the initial class is to prepare and carry out activities for a nursery school program that is operated within the high school and supervised by the Child Development teacher. After a year of supervised day-care responsibilities, students may volunteer at a local day-care center or a nursery school, putting into practice what they have learned. As students become more confident in working with children, they may progress to a day-care job, supervised by their teacher, where they earn school credits and a paycheck.

Students in Advanced Child Development complete an individual portfolio, which contains their resumé, three lesson plans for different kinds of activities with appropriate resource material, certificates, evaluations, letters of recommendation, photos of themselves working with children, and other pertinent material. These portfolios become a tool for job interviews and college applications.

Each advanced student also writes and produces a children's book, using cardboard, contact paper, laminating film, and other supplies. The finished products that I observed looked remarkably professional. The students add these books to their portfolios.

The Child Development course encourages students to consider college. As an exercise in the final class, students complete an application to the local community college, which has a training program for day-care workers. Most of these students would not have chosen to go to college; but many begin to see college as a logical next step, and they often enroll.

Other Features that Encourage Excellence

Eleanor Roosevelt is not paradise. Teachers teach six periods a day, while their colleagues in the surrounding districts teach only five. The year before my visit, they received no raise and the school closed for five and a half days, forcing the teachers to have a furlough with no pay. Teachers and administrators often serve as teacher substitutes to save money.

In spite of these shortcomings, most teachers would rather teach six periods a day at Eleanor Roosevelt than five periods at another school because they believe that they make a difference in their students' lives. They are proud of the work they do and of the innovative programs that help students of all abilities.

Eleanor Roosevelt's principal, Dr. Gerald Boarman, works hard to create an ethos of collegiality. He believes it is important for teachers to share experiences and spend time together. For example, one year the English teachers went to the National Gallery in Washington, D.C., during the school day, where an art expert taught them how to "read" a painting. Another time they viewed original manuscripts at the Folger Library. While the teachers are away, Dr. Boarman makes sure their students also have a special activity. When the math department was away recently, for instance, their students attended an AIDS awareness assembly in place of math class.

A variety of programs address similar needs for collegiality and empowerment among students. Following are several examples:

A strong *student government association* meets daily as a class and offers social studies credit to participants. They learn about parliamentary procedures and aspects of the school operation. The student government is in charge of homecoming and various fund raisers, but it also takes a stand on community issues. When the Board of

Education cut funding for schools, association members protested by camping overnight in the school, along with many of their parents. They spent the night discussing school issues and their options in confronting the board, making the experience a positive one.

Foreign language study involves nearly 70% of the students in learning French, Spanish, German, Latin, Russian, Italian, or Japanese. All may be studied for four years. Out-of-district students often enroll at Eleanor Roosevelt in order to study a foreign language that is not available in their home district. Both German and Japanese students participate in sister-school arrangements and visit their respective countries in alternate years.

The *hearing impaired program* provides interpreters for deaf students, most of whom are mainstreamed. Other students often take notes for the deaf students, who must lip read as teachers talk. Hearing students may take a course in sign language taught by a deaf teacher. The course is so popular that the school offers six sections. All major events, from school plays to graduation, include a signer for the hearing impaired.

The *arts* flourish at Eleanor Roosevelt High School. There are three concert bands, a symphonic band, three orchestras, jazz and Dixieland bands, and a flute choir. Singers may choose among a chamber choir, a women's choir, a men's choir, a concert choir, a gospel ensemble, and a barbershop group. Many student musicians study with members of the military service bands or the National Symphony.

Eleanor Roosevelt High School excels by matching the diversity of the student body with a diversity of opportunities for both students and their teachers.

Whitney High School

Whitney High School is located at 16800 Shoemaker Avenue, Cerritos, California 90701. Telephone: (310) 926-5566, ext. 2400. The principal at the time of the Blue Ribbon award was Dr. Pauline Ferris.

Whitney High School, 7:55 a.m.: Students are sitting on the floor in the halls, doing homework, chatting, and reviewing notes. The principal, Dr. Pauline Ferris, begins her morning rounds. "Let's go, Whitney scholars, time for class," she urges good-naturedly. She stops to chat with one youngster about a class in which he's been having difficulties, with another about trying out for the baseball team. She asks a third about her mother, who has been ill.

The faces of the students who respond to Dr. Ferris belong to a broad mix of ethnic and racial backgrounds. More than 60% of Whitney's students are Asian in origin: Korean, Indian, Chinese, and Filipino. Whites, Hispanics, and African-Americans make up the remainder. While schools across America are discussing multicultural diversity, Whitney is living it in suburban Cerritos, 30 miles south of Los Angeles. The community is made up of low- to upper-middle-class families, nearly 70% of are minority.

Celebrating Diversity

The students of Whitney High are proud of their ethnicity. Korean, Filipino, and other ethnic clubs celebrate their heritage; but no club's membership is exclusive. A close look at any given club reveals a mixture of whites, Asians, and African-Americans. The clubs attract students with unique activities. Many join the Filipino club because they are interested in ethnic dance, for example.

Each year the school holds an International Day. Every ethnic group contributes its specialty foods, puts on dance demonstrations, holds a fashion show with native costumes, or in some way models a unique aspect of its culture.

Ethnic parent groups abound as well. Many of the families are new to the United States; and the Whitney office regularly receives telephone inquiries from Australia, Taiwan, Spain, and elsewhere. Word has spread, especially in Asia, that Whitney is a place where students will be well-educated. Families often move to Cerritos so that their children can attend the school. Unfortunately, students are not guaranteed admission.

Whitney is an academic magnet school of 1,000 students with a waiting list of 600. The school has a single mission: to prepare every student for college. Students are accepted after passing an entrance examination and a writing assessment. Most new students enter in grade seven, giving them two years of junior high school to hone their skills before taking on the rigors of the high school courses.

Support for Students

Once students are accepted, they become part of the "Whitney family"; and the school staff gives them every possible kind of support. For example, during the summer before they begin at Whitney, incoming seventh-graders participate in a two-week study-skills class. They focus on how to take notes, how to study, organizational skills, and time management. They will need every skill, since all courses at Whitney are taught at an honors level, with many Advanced Placement selections.

During orientation, each incoming seventh-grader, as well as every other new student, is assigned a big brother or big sister, whose job is to help the younger student succeed at Whitney. Many seniors take pride in being mentors for the newcomers.

Support for the seventh-graders includes a core team of seventh-grade teachers that meets together regularly. Their purpose is to identify students who are having difficulties, to share information about those students, and to develop intervention strategies to help the students find success. The Whitney staff is always alert to students who become at risk of school failure. They consider all seventh-graders to be at risk, because these students are embarking on a new educational experience at a difficult school.

As the year progresses, any student with a 2.5 grade point average or below is put on academic probation for two semesters. Teachers, older students, and counselors then concentrate on assisting that student. After two semesters, a committee reviews the student's progress. A few students on probation decide to leave Whitney and return to their neighborhood high schools. But if the teachers and parents agree and the student wants to stay, even though the student's grades are still poor, then a faculty member "adopts" the student.

The adopting teacher maintains constant contact with the student. They chat, have lunch together, and meet often so that the teacher can review assignments and work with the student. The teacher also keeps in touch with the parents. So far, no "adopted" student has ever failed to succeed at Whitney.

Other avenues also are open to students with academic needs. They may sign up for a peer tutor. Any day after school, the classrooms and halls are filled with pairs of students and tutors, reviewing new concepts, checking out homework, and discussing course content.

Another option for students experiencing difficulties is to ask for a PAL (Peer Assistant Leader), who has been trained for a semester in dealing with troubled students. There are 15 to 25 PALs each year. Having teachers or older peers reach out to them often makes the difference between failure and success for younger students.

Early in the spring semester, another support is added. Many teachers begin after-school study sessions where they reinforce study techniques, review study skills, and supervise homework. These positive reinforcements help to strengthen marginal students' ability to learn.

The teachers at Whitney actively seek to create the best learning environment possible. They are well-qualified, bright, and enthusiastic about the school and the students. They are willing to work late with special groups or to tutor individual students. They try new teaching techniques and look for ways to make their classrooms more pleasant and more conducive to learning. Several faculty members commented to me that in most classrooms with traditional seating arrangements, little learning goes on farther back than the third row. Consequently, instead of rows, they create alternative seating arrangements that foster collaborative learning and enable the teacher to interact more effectively with the students.

Experiences in Democracy

Whitney considers itself to be a microcosm of American culture. It attempts to practice the values of society at large. School and club constitutions, for example, mirror the Constitution of the United

States. A remarkable Whitney tradition is its replication of the electoral process.

The school election campaign begins with a voter registration drive. Students running for office make speeches seeking support. The school borrows a polling booth from the Cerritos City Council, and the student body votes for members of the electoral college. Then, for an entire day, the school holds an electoral convention. Students represent all 50 states and make speeches as they commit their votes to different candidates. When the day is over, they have new student council officers — and an increased awareness of the American electoral system.

Whitney students also study the functions of the United Nations through a ninth-grade history course in which they create a Model U.N. Students study current issues and represent countries in the Security Council, the General Assembly, or special committees. They become knowledgeable about such issues as global warming, nuclear weapons, and terrorism in order to debate effectively. Once a year they participate in a shared Model U.N. with students from other schools.

It is useful to keep in mind that Whitney accomplishes these programs in a minimal physical plant. The school does not even have a cafeteria. In good weather the students have lunch outside on the ground or on benches, and when it rains they sit in the hallways to eat. There is neither a gym nor an auditorium, so plays and indoor athletic events must be held at other locations. A group of students successfully negotiated to hold their graduation exercises at the new Cerritos Performing Arts Center.

In spite of limited school facilities, there is no shortage of student involvement. Ninety percent of the students participate in a club or athletic activity. The school does not sponsor football but does field a large marching band. Students can choose among five classes in dance, for which they can receive credit in either physical education or fine arts. An eager actors' group puts on performances several times a year. The fine arts teacher encourages students to explore the resources of her studio and helps them find new artistic experiences.

Sharing Decisions

One reason that the students and staff are so enthusiastic about Whitney is that they share in making decisions about the school. Dr.

Pauline Ferris is a strong, effective principal with a clear vision of the school's mission. She believes that mission will be attained only through sharing decisions.

The Student Council, whose officers meet daily during a class period, plans fund raisers, dances, and community service projects. It organizes and conducts the new student orientation. It also approves plans for certain school activities, club constitutions, and purchase-order requests from clubs.

The students who serve on the Principal's Advisory Board give the principal feedback on courses, the class schedule, and practices that they feel need to be changed. The year before my visit, they lobbied successfully for a new Advanced Placement Physics class. Students also are active participants in the Parent-Teacher-Student Association; and one student serves as a Board of Education representative, acting as a liaison to the Student Council.

New curriculum ideas usually are generated by the teachers. Including the Model United Nations in the social studies curriculum was suggested by the staff member who now teaches the program. The science staff proposed a new environmental science class, which is now on the schedule. Faculty members decided that regularly discussing the seniors' progress might forestall student problems. They formed a senior core group that now meets routinely over lunch to review twelfth-graders' achievements and crises.

When a new teacher is hired, a master teacher always volunteers to be a mentor to the new staff member. Mentor and newcomer observe each other in class and frequently have lunch together to share ideas. In fact, regular staff members often observe one another. "Observing and giving feedback is a good way for teachers to grow professionally," says Dr. Ferris. "Teachers who are afraid to be observed are usually working too much in isolation and need to overcome their fear of assessment. Evaluation should be used as a means of improving instruction."

Sometimes sharing begins informally. A new teacher I spoke to during my visit had no classroom of her own and so moved from room to room each period. A veteran English teacher set up an extra desk in her own classroom and offered to share space with her new colleague. Room sharing led to mutual observations, coordinated lesson planning, and some team teaching.

A strong stake in the school and the students helps teachers feel comfortable giving extra time to the students. More than one teacher told me that they give students their home telephone numbers so that students can call if they have a problem with an assignment. "We don't allow a student to become invisible," commented one teacher. "We're proud of the school and willing to accept a lot of responsibility for the youngsters."

Secretaries also show the same kind of care for students. And the students are appreciative. Once a year on Secretary's Day, the students hire a limousine to drive the secretaries to a local restaurant, where they are treated to lunch while student volunteers answer telephones at school.

Parent Involvement

Parents are enthusiastic about the school. One mother told me, "Whitney presents a fantastic opportunity for a child who can meet the entrance requirements. We have none of the problems of other schools; it's a safe, secure environment. My son is learning."

"They're not all that intelligent," said another parent. "But they're all motivated. That makes the difference."

"I'm jealous of my daughter's study habits," commented a father. "She's better organized than I am."

Parents have formed the Whitney Foundation for Educational Excellence, raising money for the school through contributions from local businesses. The foundation buys needed items. For example, when a science class was short of textbooks, the foundation purchased the additional books.

Whitney's success is evident at the end of the school day, since many students stay at the school. Students stay for athletics or clubs. They stay to tutor or be tutored. And some just sprawl in the halls to do their homework and chat. The last administrator to leave in the evening must make sure that all the students have gone home.

Being part of this diverse family is important to the students. One twelfth-grader summed it up clearly: "I'm looking at several colleges," he told me. "I want to be challenged intellectually, but there's another important criterion. I'm looking for a school with a racial balance like Whitney's — I don't want everyone to be the same."

That struck me as an important thought for the 21st century.

South Brunswick High School

South Brunswick High School is located on Major Road, Monmouth Junction, New Jersey 08852. Telephone: (908) 329-4044. The principal at the time of the Blue Ribbon award was Richard A. Kaye.

South Brunswick township is not a place where one might expect to find new educational ideas. Until the late 1950s, when big developments began, the township consisted mostly of farmland. Today South Brunswick is a growing New Jersey suburb, located midway between New York and Philadelphia. Residences range from $450,000 estate homes to trailer parks. South Brunswick is heterogeneous racially as well as economically. Since the township is made up of several very small towns, the high school is the real center for the community.

Each year South Brunswick High School sends about 50% of its graduating seniors to four-year colleges and another 20% to community colleges. The rest enter the working world. Therefore, the school must provide strong vocational as well as college preparatory courses.

Astonishingly, this small suburban high school boasts one of the largest and most successful experiential learning programs in the United States. The program is called Community Involvement in Personal Educational Development (CIPED). It requires every high school junior to spend time in the community, either giving service or exploring a career.

Community Involvement Through Volunteerism

Students, educators, and parents have long recognized the need to bridge the gap between the learning experiences of the classroom and the applied skills of the workplace. CIPED gives students an opportunity to work as an intern alongside an adult mentor in order to learn skills and behaviors that are appropriate in the workplace.

All students take a career course designed to help them look at their values, skills, and interests and to discover the kinds of jobs most compatible with them. Then, at the end of their sophomore year, the students select an area for CIPED placement. Opportunities abound because the school is located between Princeton and Rutgers Universities and between the state capital in Trenton and the county seat in New Brunswick.

Students obtain placements in universities, day-care centers, schools, hospitals, theaters, museums, newspapers, government agencies, and large and small businesses, from Johnson & Johnson and IBM to the local car repair shop. Many students choose a site related to their career interests; but some choose to volunteer in the community, instead of sampling a career.

Principal Richard Kaye encourages the service option. As he told me, "We have to help young people understand that the community nurtured them. They have a responsibility to return something to that community, so we have something to build upon for the next generation."

Wednesdays at South Brunswick High School are for CIPED. Every junior leaves the school at 9:30 each Wednesday to spend the rest of the school day in exploration, adventure, and challenge. This schedule has allowed the school to create some exciting new ways for juniors to serve the community, besides the traditional types of placements. An example is the PUSH program, which stands for Prevention Using Student Help. For the past four years, some CIPED students have participated in PUSH, in which they teach a drug education program to sixth-, seventh-, and eighth-graders throughout the township. Teenagers, besides giving the younger children information, serve as role models. When a 17-year-old boy says to a sixth-grade boy, "I'm cool and I don't use drugs," that statement has a greater impact than any antidrug comment by a teacher.

Some students combine career learning and service. The student who hopes to become a doctor or a nurse learns much by volunteering in a hospital, as does the future teacher by assisting in a classroom. A small group of future artists spends one day each week working on their portfolios under an art teacher's supervision. The program gives them an extended time, rather than single class periods, to complete their goals.

CIPED gives students opportunities to grow in other ways as well. Choosing and following their own individual plans helps them to become self-reliant and self-confident. CIPED counters peer pressure by sending students out individually, thus helping them to become more independent and increasing their ability to relate to a variety of people. As a result, the adults they meet often become mentors.

When students were asked about their mentors during a year-end evaluation, some of their comments were revealing. Twenty-six students said they talked to their mentors about everything — college, family, school, careers, etc. Twenty said their mentors were there if they had a problem. One student commented, "He helped me turn my ideas into reality." Another said, "He inspired me; I should do my best, whatever my job."

CIPED provides real advantages in career development. Several years ago, one girl was interested in research chemistry. She assisted a chemistry professor at Rutgers who found her to be so bright and helpful that when he published a paper at the end of the year, he included her name on it. When she entered Rutgers a year later, she knew many professors and understood their work; and they knew and valued her as well.

Other successes are just as dramatic. A marginal student on the verge of dropping out thought he would enjoy selling shoes. He accepted a CIPED placement at a local shoe store. He communicated well with the manager and other employees; he liked the work. As a result, his life came to have more meaning. He developed new goals and not only completed school but was hired as assistant manager of the store after graduation.

CIPED remains a controversial program, largely because juniors at South Brunswick High School attend only two class periods on Wednesdays. Some parents complain that their children are being shortchanged educationally. The colleges do not agree with them. Moreover, some of the most prestigious institutions are the most supportive of CIPED. The assistant director of one of the most competitive universities in the United States told me: "We support the CIPED program. The opportunities it presents are many and varied, allowing students hands-on experience, better understanding of career options, experience with the real world, personal growth, a chance to serve the community."

Project Promise

A variety of other programs and approaches are helping South Brunswick students. Spurred by concern over dropouts — and potential dropouts — South Brunswick initiated Project Promise 15 years ago. Project Promise is an alternative program for up to 40 students in grades 10 to 12. Four teachers operate the program out of a trailer on the school grounds. Students choose the program or are recommended by a teacher or counselor; parents must approve the decision.

Class size in Project Promise is small, permitting close teacher-student relationships. One teacher is also a certified guidance counselor. Project Promise classes are less formal than regular classes. In some of the classrooms, students find a pot of coffee, bread for toast, peanut butter, and jelly.

Attendance is a serious matter. Students use a buddy system; one student checks with another each morning to ensure that both get to school on time. Students who skip are called on the telephone; sometimes teachers drive to the homes of absent students to bring them to school. Each month the students with perfect attendance enjoy free pizza for lunch. At the end of the year, the two students with the best attendance are taken to dinner at an elegant local restaurant.

The Project Promise students tend to be teens who have done poorly in or avoided physical education classes. Therefore, Project Promise includes a group adventure one morning each week. Both teachers and students participate. They may go bowling or skating or swim at the local YMCA. The activity becomes a time to share an experience, discuss problems, and exercise.

The Project Promise school day ends at noon, since a longer day has proven to be unproductive. Instead of afternoon classes, all the students are expected to hold a job. Teachers help them to find one when necessary. Many of the students need to earn money because they come from dysfunctional families that may not provide even basic food and clothing. I learned about one girl who lived with an alcoholic mother, a grandparent with Alzheimer's disease, and a younger brother who needed care. She worked after school to support the family, then came home to cook dinner and look out for her younger brother.

Juniors in Project Promise may participate in the CIPED program, just as the rest of the students do. Last year one of the students asked to assist in a kindergarten class at her neighborhood elementary school.

She was an excellent classroom aide. The kindergarten teacher became an important adult in her life, one with whom she began to discuss her problems and goals. Instead of getting an after-school job like the other Project Promise students, she returned to the kindergarten each day at noon to help in the class. When an after-school job supervising children in a recreation program at the elementary school opened up, the kindergarten teacher recommended her. She got the job and did well. Although nobody in her family had ever completed high school, she began to consider a future as a teacher.

Teachers and students become a kind of extended family in Project Promise. Many of the students would probably have dropped out of school without the support and encouragement of their dedicated teachers. Instead, a few go directly to the local community college; others try college a year or two after high school graduation. Most enter the working world and function well. They know they must arrive on time and get to work regularly if they want to keep a job. Project Promise is expensive because of its low faculty-student ratio, but the expense pays off for students who stay in school with the promise of a productive future after graduation.

Teen Center Services

What happens to our students when the school day is over? The motivated, involved students are no problem; they join clubs, participate in sports, work, or occupy themselves in other positive ways. But what about the less-motivated student?

South Brunswick High School was fortunate to receive a grant from the University of Medicine and Dentistry of New Jersey, which allowed the school to employ four full-time social workers through School Based Youth Services. Additional counseling is now available to students and their parents, and several new programs have been started. The social workers lead ongoing group discussions about physical and mental health. A part-time career counselor assists students who are looking for jobs. The service also operates a campus health center staffed by a nurse with a consultant family physician.

Most significant, the school now operates a Teen Center three evenings a week during the summer and two afternoons after school during the school year. It is open to all township teenagers, from the high school, the middle school, and private schools. The center provides games, sports, a lounge, an art studio, computers, projects, rap groups, and tutorials year-round, as well as summer trips. It gives teenagers a supervised place to be, with interesting things to do and needed help with homework. In the informal setting of the Teen Center, the students also establish closer and more comfortable ties with teachers.

Many schools would find the expense of hiring the social workers prohibitive, but the Teen Center itself is not expensive to run. The school already owns the computers and the athletic equipment; it only needs to pay some teachers to be in the building for the extra hours. Most of the activity planning is done by the students, who take great pride in their Teen Center.

Another program created by the School Based Youth Services is a cross-age tutoring program. Annually a group of ninth- and tenth-graders are hired as tutors and are trained to work with younger children. Then, for two afternoons a week after school, a group of low-achieving children from one of the township elementary schools is bused to the high school to work with the tutors. Each teenage tutor pairs with an elementary youngster. The tutorial always ends with recreation or arts and crafts and a snack. The tutorial program has been effective both academically and interpersonally. The positive relationships between younger and older children have come to be an important part of their lives. Local businesses now pay the salaries of the teenagers and the supervising teacher.

STEP Program

Another group of students is potentially at risk after graduation: special education students who are severely impaired. At South Brunswick High School the Special Training and Employment Program (STEP) is designed to help these students. The STEP program finds part-time jobs for the students while they are in school. A special education teacher works on job-related skills in the classroom and then supervises the students at their work sites. She sees difficulties that arise and works with her students to overcome them. After they graduate, many of the students move into their jobs full time and become productive members of society.

Employers have been enthusiastic about these students. For example, when a large business has a staff cafeteria, someone is needed to clean the tables and load the dishwasher. Most people who take such menial jobs grow bored with them quickly and soon look for another job. The special education students take pride in work they can do well, are happy to be earning a salary, and seldom miss a day of work.

The STEP teacher continues to meet monthly with the students after they graduate. She is able to help them with problems at the work place and in setting new goals for themselves. Sometimes she assists them, with support from their families, in finding new living situations in group homes or, occasionally, in an apartment of their own.

South Brunswick High School is far from perfect. In the sluggish economy of recent years, the school budget has occasionally been defeated by the voters. Teachers sometimes become discouraged. But the mood in the school generally is upbeat.

The programs I observed have made the school more productive and more relevant to South Brunswick students. After Project Promise was put into effect, the yearly dropout rate decreased, attendance improved, and students' self-esteem soared. The special education students move confidently into the working world when they graduate. South Brunswick has become a more friendly community than it once was; and teenagers volunteer to help those in need, whether younger students or community adults.

Craftsbury Academy

Craftsbury Academy is located at P.O. Box 73, Craftsbury Common, Vermont 05827. Telephone: (802) 586-2541. The principal at the time of the Blue Ribbon award was Richard A. Shanley.

The graduating class at Craftsbury Academy numbered only 15 students. Four hundred people came to graduation; some of them didn't even know anyone who was graduating. The academy is the center of life in Craftsbury, a small rural town in northeast Vermont. Most adults attended the school, and everyone in town participates in its events. When the basketball team made it to the playoffs of their division in the state championships, the entire town emptied because everyone made the hour-long drive to Barre for the big game.

Craftsbury today has a population of about 600 people, roughly half the size that it was 100 years ago. In the 18th century the area was so heavily forested that roads and railroads came late to this part of Vermont. Ethan Hubbard, former director of the Vermont Historical Society, commented, "A squirrel could go from Plymouth Rock to the Mississippi River without touching the ground."

Craftsbury students — 140 in grades 7 to 12 — attend classes in the oldest public school in Vermont. The building was erected in 1829. Small is considered beautiful in this rural town, but it has both advantages and disadvantages for students. "If you have a problem, all the teachers help you because they know everyone," boasted one student. "But we never get to meet anyone new," complained another.

Craftsbury's small size enables students to have many unusual learning experiences. Each year, two goals for the school are set; both teachers and students work to implement them throughout the year. The goals are posted in each classroom to remind everyone of their importance. Several years ago one of the schoolwide goals was for everyone to spend more time reading, and so a 16-minute silent reading period was scheduled in the school day. The reading time was utilized so effectively that it was added permanently to the schedule. Every day, at the beginning of school, both teachers and students read. Sometimes, when class begins, adults and teenagers share their thoughts about the books they currently are reading.

The year I visited the school, one of the goals was that all school members would be involved in a community service project. A number of initiatives have resulted from this goal. Some of the students now visit a local nursing home in order to talk to the residents. The National Honor Society members each have adopted a younger student who has some unmet needs, making contact with them at least once a week. The National Honor Society also invites townspeople, such as retirees, to a luncheon or a tea each year. The guests visit classes, attend an Honor Society meeting, and then have a guided tour of the building.

Thematic Trips

An experience that is made possible by the school's small size is a yearly thematic trip by the entire student body and faculty. The themes have been narrow, such as learning about whaling, as well as broad, such as learning about Canada. Before embarking, about five school days are spent in developing skills or acquiring information for the trip. The students meet in cross-age, heterogeneous groups, which also is how they travel. Students enjoy planning with other youngsters of different ages and from different classes. They also see their teachers in a new way. Teachers usually teach outside their specialty for the trip, and so create their own learning experience. Principal Dick Shanley, for example, taught survival French for the Canadian trip; an English teacher taught the metric system.

Decisions about the project are made democratically, with the entire school functioning as a town meeting. Teachers suggest possible themes, and students are free to add to the list. The school then breaks into small mixed groups that include students of all ages and abilities. Each group selects a leader and a recorder. After discussing the possible themes, the group votes and records its opinions. The groups then report their decisions to the entire school; a computer is used to tabulate the data.

When the theme has been decided, preparations begin. A recent destination was the Adirondack Mountains in New York State. Among the preparatory events were visits by a Native American who demonstrated basket weaving and a geologist who talked about land formations. The school also created a display of Adirondack furniture and read stories about the Adirondack people.

The trips last from two to four days. Sometimes the entire school goes together, as they did on a whale watch. For other trips they may form smaller groups. Several groups, each taking a different excursion, were formed for the Canadian trip: one to Quebec, one to Prince Edward Island, another backpacking in the Gaspee Peninsula.

The trip activities should have an educational value, though students have a great deal of latitude in what they choose. Besides the learning and the fun, the students also take pride in sharing ideas with schoolmates of different ages. As a seventh-grade girl commented, "I bet there aren't many schools where seventh-graders and twelfth-graders are able to have a good time together."

The trips are expensive, but the school raises the money through endless spaghetti suppers and several "Super Bingo" evenings. Sometimes the students must make difficult choices. One year they wanted to travel in the comfort of a rented bus instead of a school bus. It meant extra spaghetti suppers to cook, and then camping instead of staying at an inn; but the decision was made by the students and respected by the faculty.

Regular physical education trips away from the school also are high points that are made possible by the small school population. They take place several times a year. On these occasions, the school closes at noon; and teachers and students pick an activity for the afternoon. One recent winter afternoon, the choices were downhill skiing, cross-country skiing, back-country skiing, snowmobiling, ice skating, or swimming at an indoor pool in a nearby town. Students enjoy sharing these informal activities with their teachers. Since Craftsbury is in northern Vermont, with heavy annual snowfall, the winter sports are especially enticing.

Distance Learning

The curricular disadvantages of such a small school are all too evident. With a graduating class of 15 to 20, Craftsbury cannot offer the variety of courses found in larger schools. But the school compensates in many creative ways. For example, physics and chemistry are offered in alternate years so that all college-bound juniors and seniors can take them at the same time.

The only foreign languages offered are French (the school is only two hours from Montreal) and Latin. However, a satellite dish was donated to the school, enabling students to participate in a variety of programs from around the country through distance learning. Recently a group of students wanted to study Spanish, and a community adult also was interested in learning the language. Every afternoon the adult arrived at 1:30 p.m. with her small daughter. A student from the Home Economics Family Life course then picked up the little girl and looked after her for 45 minutes. The mother became the informal teacher. She and the six students watched the program together, repeating phrases and holding conversations. Using the study guide, the mother then assigned homework and monitored tests. People fluent in Spanish also came to converse with the students. Language tapes were available for students to borrow if they needed extra practice.

Another problem is that the student body is too small to offer Advanced Placement courses. But here again distance learning offers options. For example, the satellite dish picks up a course in Advanced Placement Calculus offered by the University of Oklahoma. When one math student decided to take it, he bought the textbook and tuned in to the class every day. One of the math teachers at the school became his mentor, and they met weekly to discuss the work. The University of Oklahoma has an 800 telephone number so that he could call in if he had difficulty with an assignment, and a graduate student in Oklahoma would discuss the student's question. The student completed weekly quizzes under the supervision of the mentor, faxed them to the university for grading, and quickly received the results by fax.

Encouraged by the math student's success, one girl at Craftsbury now takes Advanced Placement Biology by satellite. She uses much of her conference time with her mentor to complete the labs.

The limited number of courses that Craftsbury is able to offer sometimes means that seniors have few subjects from which to choose. Some seniors select a work-study experience to complement their classroom learning. One senior who hopes to become a chef signed on as an apprentice to the chef at a local inn. A future journalist worked at a newspaper to expand his knowledge of his anticipated career. Some teenagers simply select a course, such as world literature, and study independently, assisted by a teacher-mentor who meets with them weekly.

Faculty teach six daily classes and also assume responsibility for other activities. The community is poor, and its teachers are among the lowest paid in Vermont. But they stay because being part of a strong, caring institution offers intrinsic rewards. Many of them also attended the school, as did their parents; and they enjoy being part of this close-knit community.

Empowered Staff and Students

The staff makes major decisions about curricula and class schedules. Recently a science teacher and a math teacher scheduled their classes back to back. Sometimes they teach independently, and at other times they merge their classes for interdisciplinary activities. Seventh- and eighth-grade English teachers have chosen to teach a double period for language and literature, which gives them a longer period of time for reading and writing experiences.

Social studies, home economics, and art teachers come together for cultural units. During a unit on Japan, a Japanese student from a small college in Craftsbury came to an art class and showed the students how to write their names in Japanese characters. The students then carved their Japanese names on an eraser to make a stamp. They also did origami (paper folding), made fish kites, and read haiku. In the related home economics and social studies classes, they cooked Japanese food, learned about Japanese culture, and practiced mapping skills related to Japan.

A few of Craftsbury's teachers are leaders in new teaching techniques. Joan Simmons, who teaches English, is a prime example. Her students were creating portfolios several years before the national movement took hold. They choose samples of their work for the portfolios and must justify their choices, thus learning a great deal about critical selection and organization in the process. Keeping portfolios also enables them to see if they have taken risks in their writing and if they have improved their skills. Students often share their writing with a class by reading samples aloud.

Administrators and teachers also are comfortable permitting the students to make many decisions about school life. A student advisory council meets regularly with Principal Shanley to discuss both school strengths and problems. Last year the students were concerned about smoking in the bathrooms. The advisory council campaigned successfully to institute appropriate punishment for the students who were caught smoking and to initiate an educational program on the effects of smoking.

The student council is similarly active. Prompted by concern about school spirit, they plan and conduct pep rallies and a winter carnival. They also meet frequently with the principal to discuss school issues.

Parents and other community members participate actively in the operation of Craftsbury Academy. The parent who guided the Spanish class is one of many adults who volunteer in the school. Volunteers help to staff the school library and work with students to put out the school newsletter. Each year several parents take the thematic trip with the school. Much of the work for which other schools have to pay is done by volunteers in Craftsbury.

The school is small and informal, so that casual encounters are not unusual. One day during the winter, four cross-country skiers stopped by the faculty room looking for a restroom. Then they asked if there was any coffee that they could buy. Pretty soon the skiers were sitting down and chatting about education with the staff who happened to be there. To visit Craftsbury Academy is to see rural America at its best, with the school at the center of town life and the whole town involved in school affairs.

New Trier High School

New Trier High School is located at 385 Winnetka Avenue, Winnetka, Illinois 60093. Telephone: (708) 446-7000. The principal at the time of the Blue Ribbon award was Dr. Dianna M. Lindsay.

Most large high schools are concerned that incoming students, arriving from smaller and more personal institutions, will get lost in the large student population and fail to adjust to the new, complex school. New Trier High School makes a special effort to prevent new students from becoming merely "faces in the crowd."

New Trier serves more than 2,800 students. Located in a wealthy suburb 25 miles north of Chicago along the Lake Michigan shore, the school draws students from five nearby communities. New Trier is an affluent school. Its theaters, pool, music rooms, and science labs cannot be duplicated by most schools. But the most innovative aspects of the school are unrelated to its wealth. The structures that New Trier employs to help students become self-actualizing adults can be adopted by any school that cares.

Advisor System

New Trier keeps new students from getting lost in the crowd with one of the oldest and most successful advisor-advisee systems in the United States. Their program is based on the belief that a classroom teacher who sees students daily makes the best possible advisor. Every incoming freshman is placed in an advisory group of about 24 students, all of the same sex and in the same grade, with a teacher-advisor who is also of the same sex. The groups are roughly heterogeneous in terms of student abilities and interests, and the students come from a variety of sending schools. These advisory groups meet for 25 minutes at the beginning of every school day for all four years of high school.

The groups engage in many different activities. There are official responsibilities, such as taking attendance, discussing school rules, and electing representatives to various school organizations. Advisors discuss participation in sports and clubs; sometimes they help students develop service activities. And they work with freshman students and their parents to plan each student's four-year course of study at New Trier.

The informal goals of the advisory program are equally important. Students form personal relationships with each other and with their advisors. Small-group discussions and one-on-one counseling take place frequently. The groups also give students time at the beginning of each day to review homework, talk about plans for the day, and discuss problems. They offer a few unhurried moments before the pressure of the day's activities.

The advisory group is a stable, secure meeting place for every student, every day. In some advisory groups each member's birthday is celebrated with a small party in the morning. Some groups meet for pizza in the evening and then go together to a basketball game or other school event.

Advisors spend time getting to know their advisees, including making a personal visit to the home of each student before or during ninth grade. They meet the families and see the students in their home environments. The school's goal is for the advisor to become an advocate for each of the students. For instance, if a student is not doing well in math class, the math teacher's first step, after talking to the student, is to discuss the problem with the student's advisor. In that way, students benefit from a coordinated approach to intervention when problems arise.

Another important member of the freshman advisory group is the senior helper. Seniors enjoy the status of assisting freshman groups, and they become role models for the ninth-graders. Before the opening of school in September, the senior helpers always have a party for their freshmen; they welcome them to the school, answer their questions, and give them an opportunity to meet other new students before the first day of classes.

By the time students begin their junior year, the advisory groups have an added function. They are a place to discuss post-high school plans. The career/college counselors meet either with the advisors or with the entire advisory group to help students plan for college or think about jobs. In many schools, students meet with guidance counselors in order to prepare post-secondary plans; but at New Trier this process is built into the daily advisory group, so students have more time for discussion and related activities.

The advisor-advisee system draws parents into close contact with the school, especially when their children are ninth-graders. Each advisory group has one or two parent representatives. The freshman parent representatives become a Freshman Parent Group that elects an executive committee and works closely with the school.

Social Development Planning

There are many other ways in which New Trier High School tries to ease the transition to the school for incoming ninth-graders, such as meeting parents and eighth-grade students to explain courses, athletics, and other activities.

The school identifies future ninth-graders who may have difficulty in adjusting to high school. One hundred of these students go on a three-day summer camping trip, supervised by eight faculty members, before they start the ninth grade. Through this activity, they begin to bond with each other and get to know some of their teachers. The participating faculty members stay in touch with these students after school starts so that they can be available if a student needs help.

Another source of support for new students is peer helpers, older students who are trained in listening skills and group leadership. These students are available to meet with small groups of freshmen who need to talk and share concerns.

One of the important elements of easing the transition for incoming ninth-graders is parent input, which the school seeks at every step. Besides their role in the advisory groups, parents are consulted about the summer camping program, after-school clubs, and other activities. When a team of teachers creates a schedule for each freshman, it is based on input from parents, students, and eighth-grade teachers. They call parents to discuss the schedule, explaining the reasons for their choices. Parents have the right to change the schedule. However, if parents place a child in a class that is not recommended by the teachers, the parents must accept responsibility if the student has difficulties with the class.

When students enter New Trier High School, emphasis is placed on sports and clubs as well as on courses, because social development is considered as important as intellectual development. In advisory groups, much time is devoted to an exploration of these activities, of which there are many.

Of all the student clubs, the most popular and prestigious is Social Services. This club has been around for 20 years and is managed by a 38-student board of directors. The club supervises a volunteer service program that is active at a variety of sites in Chicago, as well as the North Shore suburbs. Students volunteer after school on weekdays and on Saturday mornings at soup kitchens, hospitals, nursing homes, day-care centers, and a reading center for children. A monthly excursion to an inner-city Chicago school gives the volunteers a chance to take the Chicago children on trips to museums and other places of interest. New Trier provides buses or vans, each supervised by a faculty member, to transport club members to the various volunteer sites. Approximately 500 New Trier students participate in this program.

Two faculty members advise the student directors of Social Services, but the decisions and the work are handled by the students. The directors meet the last period of every day and have many responsibilities: recruiting volunteers, keeping weekly contact with the volunteers, looking for new volunteer sites, and raising money. Transportation costs for the buses and vans are shared by the students and the Board of Education. Students raise funds with yearly events, such as the Battle of the Bands, which often grosses $25,000. In the spring the board of directors accepts applications and interviews potential new directors to replace the graduating seniors.

The volunteers earn neither credits nor money for their time. I asked several students why they chose to belong to Social Services. "I don't see people with problems in my world," said one girl. "At the soup kitchen I become aware of some of the problems in our society. When I arrive home in the evening, I'm thankful for the food on my table."

"It's exciting to see the kids at the reading center learn something new," said another girl.

"What are you talking about?" responded one boy. "How could I not take three hours a week to help other people? Some people spend three hours a day watching TV."

A girl who deals with severely handicapped children in a rehabilitation center said, "I go to see my friends. I like to be with them."

Most of these students will continue to volunteer when they leave New Trier because service has become an important part of their lives. The school reports that at least two-thirds of New Trier's graduates continue the volunteer tradition. One graduate who is now attending college in Washington, D.C., started her own project for the homeless in that city. Why have the students become so dedicated? Perhaps because they have such complete ownership of the program. They are not just carrying out the bidding of adults in the school.

Interdisciplinary Studies

Another unique contribution of New Trier High School is the work on interdisciplinary studies, which has been part of the curriculum for almost 20 years. The most frequently taught interdisciplinary course comes in junior year, when the majority of students sign up for a team-taught course in American studies, combining history and literature. The teachers use readings, films, field trips, and research to deliver instruction.

The American studies course incorporates several unifying themes. The course often has been presented as the American Dream, contrasting the ideal and the real in a chronological sequence. At the time of my visit, several teachers were using a myth-based approach. Two of these teachers, Steven Hilsabeck and Susanne Leggett, define the American myth in this way: "The core American experience is the exhortation to break away from a limiting past in a struggling ascent towards the realization of unlimited possibilities in an open and expansive future." Myths they examine include the myth of rugged individualism and the myth of endless abundance.

Instead of viewing literature and history as discrete disciplines, students are forced to see them together in a societal context. Students also learn to manage materials by creating their own texts with handouts, photos, and art work. Parents, seeing a new way to look at the American experience, often read course materials along with their teenagers.

Students in the course write research papers on topics of personal interest. One student tied issues in American education to Chicago history and found primary sources at the Chicago Historical Society. Several years ago a student interested in dance wrote about Mikhail Baryshnikov and the impact that artistic freedom in the United States made on his dancing. She sent the dancer a copy of her paper, and he responded by inviting her to see him perform when he danced in Chicago. The invitation included a backstage visit with Mr. Baryshnikov, who is rumored to have said to her, "Such a big paper from such a small person."

The many innovative programs of New Trier must be understood in the larger context of this extraordinary school. Long considered one of the outstanding high schools of the United States, New Trier offers a depth of study few schools can match. English courses include electives in journalism, creative writing, and Great Books, as well as traditional selections. In mathematics, post-calculus classes are available to students who complete calculus in their junior year, while three years of non-college preparatory math are provided for the least-able students. Science courses range from astronomy to special science sections for students who are struggling to become fluent in English. The foreign language curriculum includes Latin, Greek, Hebrew, and Japanese, as well as Spanish and French. An introductory course in language and culture is offered to students for whom traditional foreign language courses are too difficult.

The year I visited New Trier, nearly 900 students were taking one of the 18 Advanced Placement courses that are offered. Usually, 90% of the scores on the AP tests are 3, 4, or 5, thus allowing the students to earn college credit for their high school AP classes. The year previous to my visit, 12% of the graduating class were either National Merit Scholars or Commended Scholars.

Recognizing Merit

New Trier High School is one of few public schools in the United States where merit pay raises are given to teachers. The merit pay system is a source of pride to the community and confers status and financial rewards on good teachers. Beyond the normal salary scale is a level called Master Teacher. Master teachers are determined by a review committee of teachers and administrators. An even higher level, Teacher Leader, recognizes contributions to the profession beyond the four walls of the school. One of the interdisciplinary teachers, for example, is working to connect schools that are involved with interdisciplinary studies across the country by setting up conferences where they can share ideas.

When teachers prepare for evaluations, either for merit raises or as part of the traditional annual process, they are asked to write an intellectual biography, touching on their philosophy and interests in the teaching profession. This activity often proves to be a stimulating and thought-provoking experience. New Trier principal Dr.

Dianna Lindsay believes that all teachers need to expand their understanding of the pedagogy of teaching; she consistently reviews and discusses books of educational importance at faculty meetings.

Principal Lindsay brings a similar level of recognition to students through a myriad of small-scale activities that affect the school's environment in positive ways. For example, she gives students the opportunity to display their art work at school. She found a little-used hallway and converted it into an "art gallery" by lining the walls with cork board and covering a low wooden bench with carpeting to display sculpture. Exhibits are changed monthly so that many students can show their work. Often the first day of a new exhibit is planned to coincide with a performance of a play or a concert.

In fact, the arts in general are an important part of the New Trier curriculum. Visual arts classes include two levels of photography, ceramics, sculpture, and art history. Music offerings include boys' and girls' choruses, a swing choir, a concert choir, and an opera choir. There are bands, orchestras, wind ensembles, jazz ensembles, and a class in music improvisation. The dance department also offers several levels of courses, including choreography.

New Trier's outstanding programs touch on every facet of students' lives. The faculty and administration are committed not only to educating students through a comprehensive, well-articulated curriculum, but also to ensuring that the students of New Trier feel a sense of belonging — a connectedness with their teachers, their peers, and their community.

Benjamin Banneker
High School

Benjamin Banneker High School is located at 800 Euclid Street, N.W., Washington, D.C. 20001. Telephone: (202) 673-7322. The principal at the time of the Blue Ribbon award was Linette M. Adams.

Imagine walking into a school and finding students' books and other possessions sitting in the halls in front of lockers because the students did not have time to open their lockers and put their belongings away between classes. Then take into consideration the school's location in a rough neighborhood in Washington, D.C. Will those possessions be intact three hours later?

They will if the school is Benjamin Banneker High School. Thievery and vandalism are virtually unknown in the school. The students are urged to take their books out of the hall over the weekend so the floors can be cleaned.

When I asked students what they liked best about Banneker, the first thing they were likely to say was, "It's safe here." And, of course, the school is much more than safe. Banneker is truly a family for students, teachers, administrators, secretaries, and custodians. People trust each other, and visitors can sense it the moment they enter the building.

Built in 1939 as a junior high school, Banneker was transformed by 1981 into Washington's only academic magnet high school. Eighth-grade students seeking admission must make formal application, and Banneker receives transcripts and references from many junior high schools. The criteria for admission are not imposing; all applicants must read and compute on or above grade level. But the total school population is only 400 students, so there is always a waiting list for admission.

The population of the District of Columbia is predominantly African-American, a fact that is echoed in the student body, which is 97% African-American. A handful of Hispanic and Asian-American students also attend Banneker. The year I visited, there was one white student. During her application interview with Principal Linette Adams, she asked, "Will I be all right here?"

"If you're expecting to be discriminated against, you'll be disappointed," was Mrs. Adams' reply. "Everyone at Banneker is special one way or another; your difference just stands out more."

Support System

Being part of the Banneker family means that new students get support from older students and staff even before they arrive on the first day of ninth grade. Each incoming student is assigned an older student as a mentor. The mentor calls and sometimes visits the new student during the summer. Then, on the day before school opens in September, the senior class sponsors a reception for new students; part of the day is devoted to informal gatherings of mentors with their students. After that, the relationship is maintained informally to meet the younger students' needs.

Another way that new students are eased into the school is through Banneker's Summer Institute, established in 1990. For five weeks, at a time when other schools offer remedial instruction, Banneker offers a series of non-credit, enrichment courses ranging from language arts and foreign language to math and science, including field trips. About 75% of the participants are ninth-graders. Since they come from a variety of sending schools, the institute gives them a chance to get to know each other and Banneker.

As the year progresses, an astonishing array of supportive programs opens up for the Banneker students. For example, a local organization called Mentors Inc., founded in 1987 by former teacher Shayna Schneider, offers adult mentors to high school students. The year I visited the school, 54 Banneker students had a mentor, something students view as an opportunity, not a stigma. Two-thirds of the mentors are women; 60% of them are African-American; the majority are college educated. Mentors are found through presentations to such business organizations as the Chamber of Commerce, from Banneker alumni, and by word of mouth. The organization now boasts approximately 500 mentors in Washington, D.C.

The first two meetings between students and mentors take place in the high school; after that, they meet monthly and speak on the telephone weekly. The mentoring takes many forms. Sometimes, students want help with college applications and financial aid forms. They might need to learn how to dress and behave on a job interview. One girl needed an adult to accompany her as she learned to deal with public transportation in the city. They meet in homes, at the mentor's workplace, or go on trips. Often theaters, such as the Kennedy Center or the Arena Stage, donate blocks of tickets; and a group of teenagers and their mentors have an evening out.

An interesting offshoot of the mentoring program is that the teenagers who value the support they have been given often become mentors to elementary youngsters who need someone to talk to. The teen mentors use their lunch period to walk to a nearby elementary school on a regular basis and have lunch with the younger children.

During the second semester of each school year, the students receive an added academic support. Alumnae of Alpha Kappa Alpha Sorority at nearby Howard University organize tutorial sessions at the school from 9:00 to 11:00 on Saturday mornings. Teachers recommend students for these sessions; and the tutors, who are both men and women, help the teenagers to improve their work in difficult subjects.

A less formal support system is the Advisory Group, held for one hour on two afternoons a week, in which each faculty member meets with a group of students. This system replaces the typical homeroom. But the Advisory Group, with its extended time, can do much more. The students study, play games, and discuss academic and personal problems with their advisors.

The teachers also have a support system. All new teachers are assigned a mentor, a master teacher with whom they meet at least once a week and who helps them solve the myriad problems that face every new professional.

Teachers receive support from the administration as well: in dealing with students, starting new courses, and becoming part of the school's decision-making process. Administrative support also extends to secretaries and maintenance people. "I'm treated with dignity and am part of the decision-making process," the school's head custodian told me. "It's like I've died and gone to heaven."

Parents and Other Partners

Another ingredient in the Banneker success story is visibly supportive parents. They value their children's unique educational opportunities at Banneker and are willing to give their own time in order to maintain the high standards. Parents volunteer as attendance aides, assist in classes, help raise money and, in short, sell the Banneker idea.

When the school faced a crisis recently, the president of the parents' group spearheaded a campaign for Banneker. He gave time and money to the school and used his organizational skills to bring other parents to the school's aid. What is noteworthy is that the president no longer had a child at Banneker, but he wanted the school to be strong and available for other people's children.

The Banneker family and support system does not stop at the walls of the school; a number of outside organizations and individuals also are involved. Banneker was established, for good reason, a half-block from Howard University, one of the nation's largest and most prestigious African-American institutions of higher learning. The two institutions have had a partnership since Banneker's founding. Banneker students have regular access to the university library, and many of them take courses at Howard. They use the pool and the gym and hold their annual commencement exercises at the university. Although the arrangement is somewhat informal, everyone agrees that the relationship is important for both the high school and the university.

Another important partnership for Banneker is with the National Science Foundation. Members of the NSF frequently visit the school to speak to classes, provide materials, discuss career opportunities, and serve as role models for the teenagers. Students sometimes have opportunities to visit NSF-funded facilities, such as Woods Hole. One student went to Hawaii with the NSF to visit an active volcano and see the engineering feat of creating a new observatory.

One day each spring is reserved for a special visit to the school by NSF officials and guest speakers (often Nobel laureates). Fifteen to 20 NSF program managers hold small-group discussions with the students. NSF staff are rewarded by their contact with enthusiastic teenagers, and they sometimes find new ideas for funding proposals. For their part, the students have access to thoughtful — and thought-provoking — adult role models.

Breaking down the barriers between students and the adult community is important, but it takes much work and planning from the school in order create positive interactions. Pat Olmert of the NSF commented on the significance of the relationship. "Banneker has an idea for refocusing adolescent priorities to give them a picture of what adult realities are about," he says. "It's a model for the nation."

Banneker develops links to the larger community in a number of ways. For example, the school library is electronically linked with the computerized card catalog of the Martin Luther King Library in downtown Washington, which enables students to access needed research materials. Students often are assigned to do research at the many museums in Washington. A required course in global perspectives for sophomores provides an overview of modern world history from 1500 to the present. Each student is assigned one country on which to conduct research, often an obscure country such as Botswana, Rwanda, Albania, or Grenada. Part of the research that each student must complete involves a trip to a museum or art gallery that contains displays about the country and its culture.

Students also are encouraged to travel. An International Club meets biweekly to alert students to possible travel opportunities. Through the American Field Service and similar organizations, students apply for scholarships. The year I visited, two students went to Venezuela and one to Uruguay for the summer. Two other students were planning to travel to Korea, and Korean students also will visit Banneker in the future. The senior trip to Europe gives the teenagers an opportunity to see sites about which they have studied and to practice Spanish and French. Before they graduate, between one-fourth and one-third of the student body has an opportunity to visit other countries through Banneker programs.

Impromptu events can be as rewarding as those that are carefully planned. During one winter break, a New York rabbi brought a group of students from his temple to Washington. The New Yorkers linked up with a number of Banneker students, went bowling, and had lunch together, then found a place where they could sit and share stories about life in their respective cities.

Community Service

Banneker students also interact with the community in other ways. They have a long history of community service. All students are required to complete 270 hours of community service in order to graduate. Every other Wednesday, school closes early to permit them to leave for various community sites. Freshmen and sophomores usually are assigned to a site, such as a hospital or a school, where their services are needed. Juniors and seniors have more input into their placements and often choose career-related volunteer work. They may serve in one of Washington's many museums or, perhaps, work in a court where they assist the judge and other officials.

The students I spoke to expressed mixed feelings about the community service requirement. "At first I didn't see the importance at all," said one teenager. "But I learned to appreciate giving to others. I may need help some day."

Service also helps build their resumés. One girl who successfully interviewed for an excellent summer job at the Center for Strategic International Studies told me: "I had experience that applicants from other schools couldn't match: computer skills from D.C. Works, interning at George Washington University. I got the job."

National Honor Society members also perform community service. Twice a month after school, they visit Martha's Table, the local soup kitchen. They help make and distribute sandwiches. They also bring donations of clothes and toys to the soup kitchen and tutor young children who come there for meals. They then ride the van that travels around Washington, distributing sandwiches at a number of street corners.

Banneker is a curious mixture of the new and the traditional. It is on the cutting edge of educational thinking by requiring community service. There are no bells to disrupt classes; teachers just end their classes at the same time. At the end of lunch, someone simply walks through the cafeteria announcing, "Time to go." But the curriculum is a conservative one. Every student must study Latin to help with SAT preparation and with their understanding of English. Requirements are so stringent that there is room for neither substitutions nor failure in the curriculum. There are no study halls. A few students who want an extra class come to school early for an extra period.

But the teaching is anything but traditional. Teachers incorporate an abundance of discussion and small-group work where students report to each other. And the students have lots of homework. They average more than three hours of homework each night. But most students complete more Carnegie units than students from other schools in the area. They learn to get things done on time and to be on time. If students are late to school, someone calls their parents; it usually does not happen twice. I found that most students feel that the extra work pays off. All Banneker graduates are accepted in four-year colleges each year.

"This is a second home for me," said one girl. "I'm learning new things every day, and it's all right to be smart."

Their school is not beautiful; the neighborhood is not good. The extracurricular offerings are limited, and the requirements are imposing. But Banneker students know that their school is a world of learning, of growth, and of outreach — a place where they can build a bright future.

Apple Valley High School

Apple Valley High School is located at 14450 Hayes Road, Apple Valley, Minnesota 55124. Telephone: (612) 431-8200. The principal at the time of the Blue Ribbon award was James F. Boesen.

Apple Valley High School is an open-concept school, where architecture and philosophy find common ground. Principal Jim Boesen opened the suburban Minneapolis school in 1976. Knowing that many teachers are uncomfortable with classrooms that depart from the traditional "box," he hired staff cautiously.

Few walls obstruct the view of students, staff, and administrators into classrooms throughout the building. The openness is indicative of the school's philosophy of education; staff are open to new curricula, new ideas, and new ways of solving problems. Apple Valley works to eliminate the walls between disciplines and between the school and the community. The school's staff are willing to take risks, and their open attitude pays off in terms of student success.

Interdisciplinary Courses

One of the first "walls" to disappear was between disciplines. While subject areas in school typically fall into tight compartments, such as math and history, real-world problems are seldom that neat. An outstanding example of interdisciplinary teaching at Apple Valley brings together a physics teacher and an industrial technology teacher for a class combining their areas of expertise. Sometimes their students build rockets and fly them so that they can figure out altitudes and thrust. The course is hands-on, full of adventures, but crammed with learning, both about physics and technology.

A similar hands-on course brings together chemistry and food science, giving students information about the chemical nature of foods while also teaching them about food preparation. Students study how yogurt develops from a culture and then make it in the lab. They take trips to food-packaging plants and to the Food Science Department of the University of Minnesota to investigate careers in food science. An additional benefit of these courses is that there are two adults to prepare the learning activities and deal with the students, which increases the students' chances of success in the class.

When the administration and staff observed that troubled ninth-graders increasingly seemed to be falling through the cracks, they also realized that students who succeed in the ninth grade generally continue to do well throughout their high school years. Apple Valley launched a new program the year before my visit. They developed a team of ninth-grade teachers who met together one period a day to create a new ninth-grade interdisciplinary team. Now 130 students and five teachers are part of a school within a school with flexible schedules, no bells, and a great deal of integrated, thematic instruction. The teachers hope to break down the anonymity of a big school for incoming ninth-graders. Teachers get to know all the students, plan together daily, and become aware of the teenagers' problems before the problems get out of hand.

Teachers are excited about this approach for ninth-graders, and a second interdisciplinary team is being formed. Principal Boesen hopes that these new groups will become "houses away from home" for the incoming students.

Teaching in teams offers benefits to the faculty as well as to the students. The professional staff is forced to plan together, observe each other's teaching, and learn from each other. Improvement is inevitable; this is not a school in which teachers can hide in their own classrooms.

The barriers that have come down at Apple Valley do not always involve more than one teacher. Mary Weller, chair of the foreign language department, realized that successful foreign language students want to find real uses for the target language. They get bored with simple conversation and vocabulary lists and prefer to use the new language as a tool for acquiring other knowledge. As a result of this thinking, a Spanish-speaking teacher certified to teach social studies was hired; and a new Spanish Immersion Program was launched. Students now may take a double period in the class, half devoted to Spanish language and half to social studies taught in Spanish with an emphasis on Latin American culture. During the year, the students focus on ancient history, Latin American geography, and current events. Readings, discussions, and exams are in Spanish; and a Uruguayan teacher's aide makes important contributions to the class.

Sometimes teachers are afraid of change that might affect their own jobs. Starting the Spanish Immersion Program meant hiring a new teacher, because none of the other foreign language teachers was certified in social studies. The addition, several years ago, of Russian and Japanese to the foreign language offerings also necessitated hiring new staff. Some teachers already on the staff were afraid that students would stop studying the more traditional languages, such as French, because of the new "exotic" offerings. But the opposite occurred. Foreign language is now a dynamic department that moves ahead, and more students than previously have become interested in studying foreign languages. And they are studying more languages than ever before.

Mentor Seminars and Field Experience

Mentor seminars and field experience give students opportunities to move beyond the high school's resources and work with professionals in a field of interest. One trimester, two periods per day, is spent in the classroom preparing for the field experience. Students work on exercises in self-awareness, developing a knowledge of their strengths and weaknesses and focusing on individual goals. They work on research skills and learn where the resources can be found in order to follow their own interests. They also focus on such interpersonal skills as assertiveness and how to meet and greet people.

Each student then completes an individual resumé, prepares a reading list, and defines a project of interest. The school finds a mentor for each student for the next phase of the course, a supervised field experience. A student interested in animal behavior completed research on the breeding problems of Bactrian camels at the zoo, for example. Some students work with scientists at the University of Minnesota. One girl, an aspiring novelist, sent chapters as they were finished to her professional novelist mentor. All of the students write journals to explain how they use their time and send copies to their mentors in order to maintain accountability.

Not all students who select a mentor experience are high-powered learners. I learned about one student in particular, a young man named Dave. Three years earlier Dave, then a senior at Apple Valley, was in the bottom third of his class, disinterested in learning, and of great concern to his family and teachers. He had one ambition: to make

63

a clay animation film. Dave was not even successful in art classes because the classes were not doing what interested him. He signed up for the Mentor Program and went for an interview with the owners of a special effects firm that does clay animation. He was hostile and difficult during the interview, but the owners of the firm recognized behavior they had exhibited at that age. In fact, their business card bears the statement, "We're the kids your mom wouldn't let you play with." They took Dave on and he made an outstanding clay animation film. Dave developed new confidence as a result of working on the film and completed high school and two years at a community college. He now works part-time for his high school mentors.

Partnerships

Apple Valley High School has developed many kinds of connections with the community. For instance, the Minnesota Zoological Garden traditionally creates a variety of experiences for high school students. Every summer the zoo accepts a small group of students to develop projects related to animal behavior, complete research, and write the results. The students present their findings to the public at an open forum, and the zoo publishes the reports. The zoo also offers a wide variety of field trips. One day a year, for example, is Spanish day for youngsters from the entire state; Apple Valley's Advanced Placement Spanish students volunteer as guides.

The high school staff has been meeting with zoo management to plan a Zoo School for a group of eleventh- and twelfth-graders who are interested in the environment. The school will be built close to the zoo; and such subjects as math, art, and English will reflect an environmental focus. Using the zoo's resources, science will directly relate to environmental and animal behavior issues. In preparation for this undertaking, Apple Valley conducted a retreat for parents, staff, and students to discuss their feelings about the new school. A course of studies is now being prepared to show the learning sequences for students of different abilities.

After opening the Zoo School, the high school administration would like to create other specialized satellite schools, such as a school for health and human services with classrooms at a hospital.

Partnerships with local businesses are another way to open up the worlds of both the teenagers and the adults. A collaboration with Koch Oil Refinery began traditionally, with Koch helping to set up and run both a science challenge and a bridge-building event, plus offering two yearly scholarships. But the relationship recently took an interesting turn when students and faculty discovered a place in the school building where the custodians' two-way radios do not work. Nobody understands what causes the interference. Now engineers from Koch, using the company's sophisticated equipment, are working with a team of students to solve the problem. The project is a challenging one for all the participants, and it is helping to create a closer relationship between Apple Valley and Koch Oil.

Another type of community support is available to teachers in the form of Venture Grants for $500 or less. The one stipulation is that the project must be a risk-taking one. For example, the teacher of a course called Herstory, which features women in American history, received a grant last year, which enabled her to buy props and costumes so that her students could visit elementary and middle schools dressed as important women in American history. The students made presentations from the vantage point of famous women.

Many of the school's student groups also reach into the community. The National Art Honor Society, which recognizes gifted art students, is an important organization. The society is painting a mural on a wall of the senior citizens' health center. Their next project will be a mural for the post office.

Outcome-Based Education

Openness to change takes a variety of forms. Many of the teachers and administrators believe that the students are not learning enough, that the many small objectives in courses do not always lead to the grasp of large concepts. They also see multiple-choice tests as a poor assessment tool. A number of teachers, with strong support from Principal Boesen, turned to outcome-based education (OBE). Major outcomes of an OBE course are identified; if students do not meet them, they receive no grade and are encouraged to try again until they pass.

Outcome-based education is particularly effective in science courses. In past years, ninth-grade earth science students were asked to name planets, describe the phases of the moon, identify different types of rocks, and demonstrate an understanding of erosion. Now students must acquire and use new knowledge to explain such phenomena as how seasons occur. Students might be directed on a test to "explain in a paragraph why there are seasons in Minnesota, what the position of the earth is at various seasons, and how that affects climate." They must grasp the concepts in order to deal with the problem.

OBE has raised some concerns. Even though students receive grades, the traditional grading approach has been abandoned. Some parents are afraid that move will hurt their children's chances of getting into competitive colleges. Also, some students do not study and do not take the tests, feeling that there are no penalties for waiting until the second time around. That behavior creates more work for teachers and increases the burden of unmet responsibilities hanging over the students' heads. Some teachers also are uncomfortable with the concept; and while they are not forced into the mold, they feel that in order to win administrative and peer support they should be jumping on the OBE bandwagon.

Sometimes a new course starts almost by accident. Some of the members of the math team, wanting practice before a math meet, started seeing the math coach before school. The sessions proved to be challenging and motivating. Soon the math coach created a new course, Super Math, which meets every day at 6:30 a.m. "Our expectations for the kids are higher than at other schools," commented the math coach. "And we believe that academics should be rewarded just as athletics are." The course also must be fun, because everyone arrives on time each morning. Perhaps the status of being a Super Math student helps them to get out of bed early.

Apple Valley is a large school, with 2,100 students in grades 9 to 12. Sheer size allows for learning experiences not possible in smaller schools. French, Spanish, German, Russian, and Japanese are offered for four years, and the school is thinking about offering Arabic. Nine Advanced Placement courses are offered, some in almost every department. The students view their school's size with enthusiasm because they see that, besides the huge array of classes, every kind of team is available, including figure skating and ice ringette (a version of hockey for women).

The breadth of arts offerings is extraordinary, including a marching band, two varsity bands, two symphonic bands, and two wind ensembles, plus two jazz bands that meet after school. The vocal music offerings have a similar scope: three women's choruses, three men's choruses, three treble choirs, three concert choirs, and three chorales. Clearly, singing is "in" for boys as well as girls. The curriculum in dance, theater, and visual arts is equally impressive. One family recently moved from Boston to this Minneapolis suburb so that their son, a budding actor, could participate in the theater program. Concerts, festivals, and plays offer many opportunities to perform all year. The variety musical I saw during my visit was of such high quality that I could easily imagine it competing with the best on Broadway.

Few arts opportunities center on competition, however. For example, Wayne Romer, performing arts department chair, believes it is important for the band to remain non-competitive. "We need to separate the arts from the athletic mentality," he commented to me. "Competition promotes winners and losers; that doesn't fit in the arts." His marching band performs often, including the half-time show last year at a National Football League game.

Support for Marginal Students

In spite of the fact that "big is good" for most Apple Valley students, there is always the danger that "big" may allow marginal students to slip through the cracks. In 1988 the school initiated a Marginal Student Committee, and in 1990 Apple Valley became a member of the National Coalition for Equality in Learning. Both of these actions were taken to address the needs of at-risk students. Schools from across the United States hold study groups to share the problems of marginal students, which can be remarkably similar despite diverse settings. These groups discuss what the students need to survive and thrive.

Apple Valley's psychologist spearheads the school's work in this area. She points out that many schools identify at-risk students and make a plan that views them in isolation rather than in the context of the school. At Apple Valley, however, the staff look at problems that permeate the school and touch all teenagers, based on the assumption that there may be good reasons for the dysfunctional students' behavior.

One tactic in working with individual students is to identify the 10 most difficult students in a class. The staff especially focus on ninth-graders, since failure to succeed in ninth grade makes future success in school less likely. They ask these identified students, "Who can you turn to if you have a problem?" Invariably when the student names a teacher, the reason is similar: "He said I was good at math" (or English or science). This type of response moves staff to conclude that most students seek to become competent. Thus the staff work to understand their needs and help them find ways to create school success for themselves.

Apple Valley is a high school where most students succeed. They take challenging courses, earn Advanced Placement credit, and are admitted to highly competitive colleges and universities. But there also is a strong support system for those in need. "We want our students to be Renaissance men and women, who have a knowledge of and appreciation for both arts and sciences as well as a physically fit body," says Principal Boesen. Perhaps the school's greatest asset, besides a supportive community, is that attitude.

North Penn High School

North Penn High School is located at 1340 Valley Forge Road, Lansdale, Pennsylvania 19446. Telephone: (215) 368-9800. The principal at the time of the Blue Ribbon award was Dr. Juan R. Baughn.

Creative, inspired leadership can make an enormous impact on school successs. Dr. Juan Baughn, principal of North Penn High School, is such a leader. He seems to be everywhere in the school: in the corridors and classrooms, with cafeteria workers or kids or teachers. He is interested in what everyone is doing.

Dr. Baughn is a dynamic presence. Interestingly, he is the only African-American on staff in this predominantly white community high school. But he is also a reflective leader. Students and staff often approach him with their ideas for curriculum and activities for the school. Open to new ideas but thoughtful in his approach, Dr. Baughn usually responds: "Think about it and write me a proposal that I can accept." The students have learned that if they want to accomplish something, they must organize their thoughts and present them in writing.

Dr. Baughn presents himself to students as a learner. One year as part of his traditional address to the student body on the first day of school, he played a simple piano piece, having just started to study the piano. Later in the year he played a different piece, this time showing the progress he was making and demonstrating that students and adults go through the same learning process when they want to master something new.

Student Government Association

North Penn High School is a modern, attractive school with a wide variety of courses and extracurricular activities. But a concept that sets it apart from other schools is its commitment to democracy for the student body. Students at North Penn have a great deal of input into the affairs of the school through their evolving Student Government Association. The association has five officers, a cabinet, a senate, and a house of representatives, all of whom take their responsibilities seriously. The officers are elected by the student body after extensive campaigns. They then appoint a cabinet after reading applications and interviewing the candidates with their advisors. Each of the appointed cabinet members chairs a committee on topics such as educational issues or community service.

The representatives are selected from social studies classes in all grade levels; they meet monthly during the school day and maintain communications with the entire student body. The senate includes at-large representatives from each grade and the class presidents; it meets in the evenings. The senators accomplish much of the committee work.

The student council is an effective voice for the students. For example, recently the student body was upset with the school board because it continually made decisions affecting them but rarely asked their opinions. A new high school was being considered as a way to respond to the population growth; the students had ideas about the proposal. And there was talk about a new social studies curriculum, an important matter to the teenagers. The Student Government Association wrote a formal proposal to the school board, requesting a seat on the board for their representative.

At first the school board ignored the request. The teenagers, uncertain about how to follow up, showed their proposal to Dr. Baughn. They discussed what elements were most important and what compromises they were willing to make. The students then revised their proposal and presented it again. This time the school board was willing to meet with them. Together the two bodies hammered out compromises and ended by creating two student liaisons to the board. The two students have reserved seats at school board meetings and may speak first from the audience, but they do not sit with the board. The students are proud of their progress, as well as more aware of how to work within a democratic structure.

Another example of learning about democracy centered on a controversy about a talent show. By all accounts, the talent show of the previous year was a disaster. The house proposed a gong show in its place; the senate wanted to stick with a talent show. Each group proposed its own choice; they argued and voted each other down.

Controversy and anger boiled until the two groups finally met and compromised on a game show. "Democracy is not always a pretty business," explained Jim Finnemeyer, coordinator of student activities, who watched the students struggle, and learn.

Knight Crier

The *Knight Crier*, North Penn's student newspaper, is another important voice of the students. Published approximately every six weeks, the *Knight Crier* is a professional-looking paper, ranging in length from 16 to 32 pages. It covers school news, local news, entertainment, and North Penn's athletic events. In its editorials students comment on everything from President Clinton's economic policy to the school's social studies curriculum. In fact, a recent column complained about the limited role of the student liaisons to the school board and called for a "non-voting representative who can sit with board members and respond to questions directly."

"They walk a fine line," says Principal Baughn, who reads everything that is controversial after Janet Kratz, the faculty advisor, reviews it. When Dr. Baughn finds comments that he thinks are too extreme, he meets with the editors to discuss the offending passages. The students are well aware of the limitations on their power. "According to the *Hazelwood* decision," explains co-executive editor Jeremy Fiebert, "prior restraint by a principal without cause is possible." But the students also know that if what they want to print is reasonable, they probably will receive permission to do it.

Regular and advanced journalism classes are offered. Most of the editorial staff are enrolled in the advanced course, while many of the newer reporters are members of the first-year course. Several student staff members who could not fit journalism into their class schedules meet with the editors after school so that they also can participate.

In addition to offering an articulate voice for the students, the *Knight Crier* has become the focus of an exciting partnership with the community. When the articles for a given issue have been written by the students, they then are sent by computer modem to *The Reporter*, the Lansdale newspaper. After school, a quiet time for *The Reporter* staff, the students work at the newspaper office, editing articles. They get to interact with the professional journalists, use their sophisticated equipment, and learn what it is like to work at a newspaper.

71

Weekends the staff is likely to spend 20 to 30 hours at the home of newspaper advisor Kratz, completing the layout and making final revisions. When the paper comes out, the staff is exhausted but satisfied. They represent their fellow students so well that for many years the *Knight Crier* has received top awards for a school newspaper in both Pennsylvania and the United States. And the students have increased their knowledge about a career in journalism from the staff of *The Reporter*; some students even step into part-time jobs as stringers.

Reaching Out

The students of North Penn High School are exceedingly generous in reaching out to populations in need of assistance. Each year the National Honor Society hosts the Montgomery County Special Olympics at the high school, a competition for special education and handicapped students. The Honor Society students plan the event; and on the day of the Olympics each member, plus many of the other students, serves as "buddy" to a participant, greeting the participant and shepherding him or her through the many activities.

The Honor Society reaches out to other populations as well. The organization is in touch with a local elementary school, where members serve as big brothers or big sisters to youngsters who need extra help or just someone to talk to. Once a week, Honor Society students spend half an hour at the school, each with one youngster, in an activity such as reading to them or assisting with homework. They also tutor within the high school, helping English-as-a-second-language students learn English.

North Penn also supports a volunteer mentor program, in which teachers, administrators, secretaries, maintenance workers, and other adults in the school may become mentors for students in need. Who are those students? Everyone can identify this description taken from the school's mentoring handbook:

> Tom Murphy is a "C" student. Rarely in trouble and even more rarely involved, Tom moves from class to class, touching nothing. A high school specter in reverse. His body is physically present; it's his spirit that is lost.
>
> Tom receives an average of twenty negative messages a day: "You're late." "You forgot your homework." "You don't know the answer." We even tend to describe him with a series of negatives: he's not at risk; he is not gifted; he doesn't have a learn-

ing problem; he doesn't participate in extracurricular activities; he doesn't set goals for himself.

Most educators can identify students like Tom; they just don't know what, if anything, to do about him. Since he causes no problems, he gets little attention.

Each year Sue Cahill, an assistant principal who developed the program and wrote the above vignette, asks the ninth-grade teachers to give her a list of incoming tenth-graders who are potential candidates for the mentorship program. Each of the students is interviewed and asked if they would like to have an adult to work with them. Those who do, usually 50 to 75 students, are assigned a mentor.

The mentor is always someone who already knows the student. A student who is having difficulty in algebra may have a mentor who is a math teacher. One student who wanted to study Japanese but could not fit it in her schedule was mentored by the Japanese teacher. The mentoring is informal, and each mentor works differently. But all stay in close contact with their students, even after the tenth grade, to see how they are doing. Each mentor receives a small sum to spend on the student. Mentors might take students to lunch, buy them a gift, or spend it in some other way that will serve to further the mentor-student relationship.

There is no formal evaluation of the mentoring program, but both adults and students seem to be very happy with it. When I walked through the halls at North Penn, it was not unusual to hear a teacher say, "Hi, Joe, how's your paper coming? Do you need help with it?" Or, "When is that big wrestling match? I'd like to come and watch it." The mentors' goals are to help the students increase their self-esteem, participate in the school community, and increase their sense of responsibility.

Like most high schools, North Penn has a parent-teacher organization. Theirs is the PTSAO, which includes parents, teachers, students, and administrators. They meet five to six times a year in an open forum without an agenda. The members talk about issues of concern, and the students often discuss things that are happening in class. In this low-key atmosphere, they get to know each other better and often are able to resolve problems when they arise.

North Penn also supports a community education program that brings adults into the school in the evening and on weekends. Because North Penn has a swimming pool, the community members have opportunities for recreational swims, swimming and diving instruction, water aerobics, scuba diving, and water safety instruction. The school's facilities are used seven days a week, all day and all evening, to everyone's benefit.

Another important link between school and community is a career study program open to senior students, who often participate in individualized career-related placements that take them out of the building for part of every school day or for one or two days each week. A school supervisor makes periodic visits to these community placements in order to evaluate their effectiveness. One young man who evinced an interest in broadcasting, for example, is now an intern at a local radio station. He has gained career knowledge and built a relationship with professionals in his field.

Mentoring New Teachers

The North Penn students feel that they are valued members of the school community, and the school works hard to give new teachers the same feelings of acceptance and support. Each new faculty member is matched with a mentor who can be of real assistance. A math teacher, for example, would be mentored by another math teacher who is well aware of the issues and problems that the new staff member will face. According to staff developer Rick Brasch, 99% of the faculty agrees to be mentors. They do get paid for after-school hours, but he believes the intrinsic rewards of helping a new colleague are the real motivation.

New teachers begin work a week before school opens, which includes time with their mentors. Each of these teachers emerges from the orientation sessions with new skills and specific information to help with the new assignment. One outcome of a session on classroom management, for example, is that each teacher creates his or her own classroom management plan.

Susan Sinkinson, another staff developer, points out that new people in other professions can break in slowly. The beginning lawyer starts with an easy brief. But the new teacher is thrown right into a classroom to sink or swim, sometimes with the most difficult classes. Without help, some beginning teachers feel defeated and leave the field, while others have a first year of crisis, creating a poor learning environment for the children.

Having a mentor means that the new teacher can turn to an experienced professional who will observe, demonstrate, give feedback, and help the newcomer to improve. Further, the two staff developers, through personal support and a series of workshops, also act as mentors. Throughout the school year they run workshops to help the new teachers cope with such events as back-to-school nights and parent conferences. They also offer a series of credit courses on such topics as teaching styles or how to deal with disabled students.

The local community also makes teachers feel valued. A local foundation, with a community-based board of directors, raises $15,000 to $20,000 each year as educational grants for which all district teachers may apply. Recently, for example, a music teacher applied for and received a grant to bring in clinicians for a workshop with the jazz band. The young musicians had working professionals to guide them and comment on their performance for a day.

There are problems at North Penn High School. First of all, the community it serves is growing too fast. The school now houses 2,200 students in grades 10 through 12; there will be 3,000 in a few years. Class size is already over 30 in some courses. Can the school maintain its quality programs and relationships at 3,000 or 3,400 students? Would it be better to have two smaller high schools? There is no easy answer, and the question is controversial.

Compounding this problem is the lack of public transportation to link the seven towns that North Penn serves. Students who do not drive or have access to a car have trouble getting to the school in the evenings for many activities.

In spite of the problems, North Penn is a school that focuses on the personal growth of both students and faculty. It succeeds in a community that appreciates that success.

Cass Technical High School

Cass Technical High School is located at 2421 Second Ave-nue, Detroit, Michigan 48201. Telephone: (313) 494-2605. The principal at the time of the Blue Ribbon award was Dr. David L. Snead.

From the outside, Cass Technical High School looks like the antithesis of an excellent school. The building is a huge, seven-story structure in a blighted neighborhood of downtown Detroit. Inside, Cass Tech's 3,250 students are crowded into academic classes with an average of 35 students. There is no athletic field. Supplies are minimal, and the teachers do not even have the use of a photocopier.

But Cass Tech possesses something special: an *esprit de corps* that thrives on challenge. Someone once put a sign in the halls stating, " 'Can't' is not allowed to enter this building." Learning and growth are constants here.

Cass Tech is an alternative academic school. Prospective students must take an examination or have an audition in order to be admitted. Occasionally a student does not pass the examination but is able to convince the administration that he or she can profit from the atmosphere at Cass Tech. This kind of assertiveness tends to be appreciated. Teachers I met during my visit love to tell the story of a senior who had excellent grades but poor SAT scores. When she was turned down by the prestigious university she wanted to attend, she visited the university in person and convinced the admissions officer that she not only could succeed but could make an outstanding contribution to the institution. She was accepted on the spot and even offered a scholarship.

A major problem in this large school is to keep the ninth-graders from getting lost. Cass Tech works hard to be a safe haven in spite of its huge size. All freshmen must choose one of its 19 curricula even before they begin their first day of school. Each curriculum has a specific career focus and its own requirements, so that it functions as a school-within-a-school. Being part of a smaller group gives students a home base and an identification. In addition, Cass Tech has a long tradition of educational leadership in Detroit; most ninth-graders are proud to be admitted to the school.

The curricula range from Architecture to Astronautics. In addition to the general education requirements, each curriculum has its own unique requirements. Astronautics students take a number of math, computer, and science classes, plus such subjects as astro-navigation and astro-weather. Architecture students study drafting and building construction. Although most students plan to attend college, diverse career opportunities may be explored in each curriculum. An engineering student learning about motors might become a mechanic, decide to build his own garage, or go on to college to major in engineering.

The name Cass Technical High School is deceptive, since the arts are among the school's strongest programs. Visual arts offerings are extensive and include sculpture, ceramics, painting, drawing, and art composition and history. In the performing arts there are concert, marching, and jazz bands; ensembles; vocal choruses; even a harp choir. The theater department is well-established and has many famous graduates. During the year I visited the school, there were so many outstanding student actors and actresses that the school took them to Chicago for auditions with a consortium of drama schools. Dance is very popular and is a requirement for all performing arts majors. The boys enjoy the classes as much as the girls do. They have a good role model: the football coach teaches tap dance.

Internships

Students in the advanced courses often can secure internships in their fields. Detroit offers a wealth of possible experiences. Several students have been placed in the Wayne State University Molecular Biology and Toxicology Lab, assisting a researcher in developing techniques for gene splicing. One student made significant contributions in the lab and was cited as a co-author of an article on the scientist's research. Other students work in research at the Michigan Cancer Society or serve medical internships at Henry Ford Hospital. Engineering students often secure placements in the experimental engineering department of Cadillac Motors. One student, for example, worked on the problem of reducing noise from the tailpipe. Still other students have had internships with General Motors'

Saturn division, developing specifications for a clutch test, among other projects. Internships give the students an idea of the day-to-day responsibilities of professionals in their anticipated career fields and help the students decide on their future studies.

Scientific Research

One of the requirements for seniors in the Science and Arts curriculum is a course in scientific research. The goal is to teach the students how to do research through a project that may relate to a personal interest or career goal. Some of the seniors work with a mentor outside the school.

During my visit I met Tamika Tate, who hopes to become a pharmacist. She was gathering data on three childhood diseases, tuberculosis, chicken pox, and whooping cough, in order to study the effects of these diseases both on children and on society. Another student, Sargum Sood, plans to become a physician, but she was curious about her own roots in India and Africa. Her research related to the migrations of people from India to South Africa in the 1860s. Jahna Berry, who wants a career as a lawyer or a journalist, was collecting data on Asian organized crime. When I asked her why, she responded, "I like to pursue knowledge for its own sake."

Roslyn E. Kellman, the teacher of the research class, often brings her students to the library at Wayne State University to do research when the resources at Cass Tech are insufficient; and the students all have their own university library cards.

Some of the research projects have been the beginning of a major inquiry for the students. One young man interested in Spanish literature did a paper on political implications of Don Quixote. Later he received a Ph.D. from Yale; his dissertation dealt with medieval representations of culture in Spanish literature. Another student studied the copper people who lived in Wisconsin and upper Michigan 3,000 years ago. She is now completing her doctorate in anthropology at the University of Michigan; her dissertation will be on the same subject.

The classes are difficult, but being smart and working hard are the norm at Cass Tech. "Teachers here expect you to succeed," explained one youngster. "They want to motivate you, tutor you; they come to athletic events and proms. But they don't baby you; they want you to be independent."

"You look around and everyone's succeeding here. There are lots of student role models," commented another. "You want to succeed, too."

When a group of students discusses the competitiveness at Cass Tech and the importance of keeping up with assignments, the words "re-evaluate" and "prioritize" often emerge. These young people are receiving guidance in the importance of making choices between conflicting interests and goals.

Support System

For those who have difficulty with the work, Cass Tech has a strong support system. If any student's grade point average drops below 2.0, there is an automatic conference with parents and student, and tutoring is begun. Faculty always are willing to tutor a student who needs help, often arriving early in the morning for a before-school session. The National Honor Society does a great deal of peer tutoring as well, and study groups in various subjects often are formed. The school has a retention counselor who works closely with students having difficulty. His presence has made the difference with many borderline students.

One teacher, an ex-social worker, created a "We Care" program to recruit teachers to talk with students who are having academic, social, or personal problems. These teachers put a "We Care Station" sign on their doors so students will know that they can be approached in time of need. The role is particularly important because the school's guidance counselors carry exceedingly heavy loads. In spite of the support, there are always some ninth-graders who can not handle the work and the pressure; and they return to their neighborhood schools.

Environmental Studies

Cass Tech constantly seeks new ways to engage the students and to reach out to the community. Recently, for the second year, science teacher Randy Raymond was awarded an urban environmental education grant in a competition held by the National Science Teachers Association and supported by Toyota Motor Sales. Mr. Raymond had observed that the nature center at Belle Isle Park in Detroit was underused. The grant enabled him to teach environmental issues to 24 Cass Tech students, who in turn teach groups of elementary youngsters, using the Belle Isle Nature Center as a field laboratory.

The Cass Tech students visit elementary classrooms in several Detroit schools every other week, completing a variety of projects with them. Early in the year the children build bird feeders, which they take home so that they can make an inventory of the birds in their neighborhoods and gain an appreciation for their urban environment. The high school students keep journals, and the young children write about their experiences. The relationship that forms between the two groups is one of the most exciting aspects of the project. "It's fun to have someone you can really talk to when you're learning about dinosaurs and birds and stuff," commented one fourth-grader. The teenagers are as happy as the younger children with the direction of the program and have a strong commitment to maintain and expand it.

The fourth-graders have made several trips to Belle Isle. In the spring they make bluebird and wren nest boxes for the nature center. Hopefully, the youngsters will visit the center during summer vacation and see if birds are living in their nests. In addition, the children are learning to measure ground ozone and are creating their own recording devices to be used at home, an activity that can involve the entire family.

New Directions

Interdisciplinary courses are moving slowly into the Cass Tech curriculum. Recently, a group of eleventh-grade social studies, English, and math teachers decided to work together in planning their courses, even though the schedule did not permit them to work with students at the same time. Since the social studies and the English teachers are both dealing with American studies, they were able to bring the two curricula together so that students can study the interrelationships of history and literature. When students from a regular English class received the same assignment as those in the American studies group — to write a paper from the point of view of a Puritan who had come to America on the Mayflower — their papers were clearly weaker. Those papers from students in the American studies class were rich with references to history as well as to the literature being studied and demonstrated a clearer overview of the period.

The math teacher was able to complement the American studies experience. When students read Poe's "The Pit and the Pendulum," for example, he helped the students to calculate the swing of Poe's pendulum. Since one of the goals of American studies is to increase the students' ability to write well, he had them write math journals.

Another new direction for Cass Tech is an organization called Pugwash, based on a group established in 1955 by Albert Einstein to find peaceful uses for nuclear energy. The Pugwash students meet to discuss ethical questions related to nuclear energy, AIDS, and other issues. Before the discussion, each member does research on the current issue from a particular point of view, setting the stage for lively exchanges.

Two years ago the administration felt that the school should add a new foreign language to the curriculum. Since the student body is 95% African-American, they decided on Swahili to give the teenagers insights into African culture. An African teacher was found, and the program has met with such enthusiasm that there are now six sections of first- and second-year Swahili.

The *Detroit Free Press*, one of the city's largest and most respected newspapers, offers the students of Cass Tech and other high schools another unusual opportunity. Each month they turn over a page of the newspaper to Cass Tech students for use as their school newspaper. The students write the stories for the page. Then after *Press* typists have entered the material on their computers, the students in charge of layout compose the page, which is printed as part of the larger paper. The students learn about the functions of a large, professional newspaper and work with the professional journalists. The newspaper staff awakens many minority students to careers in journalism.

Principal James Snead says that his teachers create new programs because they are not afraid to take risks. The faculty is quick to point out that risk-taking is easy with an administration that encourages creativity and goes into the community to look for support.

Parents are proud to have their children enrolled at Cass Tech and are staunch advocates of the school. They volunteer to assist with such activities as the marching band and the swimming program. And there is a strong alumni group, the Cass Alumni Triangle Society (fondly known as CATS), which was organized in 1989. CATS gives food baskets to poor students' families at Christmastime and sometimes gives students money to buy sorely needed clothing.

Cass Tech is an exciting school. Classes are challenging, and extracurricular activities and sports involve many students. There is traffic into the school every day: performers, guest lecturers, and specialists running workshops. Students leave for internships in industry, courses at nearby colleges, and volunteer work in the community. The positive message is everywhere: We want to succeed, and we will.

Kennebunk High School

Kennebunk High School is located at 89 Fletcher Street, Kennebunk, Maine 04043. Telephone: (207) 985-1110. The principal at the time of the Blue Ribbon award was Dr. David McConnell.

There is a certain mystique about Kennebunk High School. Principal David McConnell, who is referred to as Headmaster, is a Kennebunk native and graduated from the school. Through a variety of jobs at other high schools and colleges during his professional career, he has always kept a house in Kennebunk and always loved the town. He returned home to head the school. Bruce Lewis, who teaches in the music department, decided when he was a third-grader in the Kennebunk school system that he would like to become Kennebunk's band director. Other faculty members were once students here, too.

Kennebunk High School, with 660 students, is a school that consistently moves forward to try new and better ways of reaching its students — but seldom without pain. Faculty often disagree over the best way to run a program, and I noticed an obvious lack of common goals. But everyone is open to improvement and growth, and there are many exemplary programs.

Ninth- and Tenth-Grade Teams

Several years ago a team approach for ninth-graders was started. A group of teachers representing English, math, social studies, and science formed a pilot team to deal with half of the incoming ninth-graders. They had rooms outside the main school building, they were not governed by school bells, and the teachers functioned as an interdisciplinary team so that they could work closely with each other and with the students. But the students felt isolated from the other ninth-graders and the rest of the school, and some of the teachers were dissatisfied.

The team concept was not discarded but modified. Now all ninth-grade teachers are part of the ninth-grade "team." They meet with the middle school teachers of the incoming ninth-graders each spring to get input for student placement. They also meet with the students and their parents to talk about the high school's program and expectations.

All of the ninth-grade teachers have a common meeting time every day. Sometimes they meet with the guidance counselors and sometimes they discuss curriculum. In particular, they are able to focus as a group on an individual student's progress. Is Joe having trouble in math? Perhaps the English teacher, in whose class he is functioning well, has an insight into the problem. Is his work slipping in all the classes? One of the teachers calls home. Does he need to be challenged more? By working together, the ninth-grade teachers can be sure that no student slips through the cracks. The ninth-graders are not assigned to a specific team, but they are aware that their teachers meet together daily and know how students are faring in each class.

In spite of abandoning specific interdisciplinary teaming, the ninth-grade classes still preserve a measure of coordination. For instance, the freshman oceanography class studies the waters off the coast of Maine, while the social studies class looks at the geography of the same area. In English class the students concurrently read a book about a young man who sails around the world and, later in the year, read *A Night to Remember*, about the sinking of the Titanic. In oceanography they inevitably discuss whether the survivors could have swum to safety or stayed on the iceberg. The students learn about the ocean water and hypothermia. The teachers work for connections that make learning relevant and interesting.

The results of the ninth-grade structure have been so positive that there is now a team of tenth-grade teachers as well. They, too, meet frequently to discuss student progress and curriculum. Their interdisciplinary work is focused on career selection. Each student completes a career research paper, and there is a sophomore career fair.

Since the grade-level team approach works so well, might it be considered for juniors and seniors? "Absolutely not," said one teacher, who went on to explain that the older students need to be more independent of the teachers in order to prepare for college and the career world.

But teaming in the older grades could focus on the process of exiting from high school, another teacher pointed out. A twelfth-grade team might help the non-college-bound students with job applications and interviewing skills and maybe even place the students in post-high school jobs before graduation. College-bound students could get help with college applications and essays.

The debate is likely to continue for some time, as that is the operative change strategy at Kennebunk.

Interdisciplinary Classes

Interdisciplinary, heterogeneous science-technology classes are another new area that receives mixed reviews at Kennebunk High School. The concept was launched when a group of technology students, all non-college-bound, needed to understand some concepts in physics in order to complete a project. So they visited a physics class of all college-bound students, and the two groups worked on the problem together. Another time, the physics students needed technical assistance in order to complete their project, and again the groups worked together. It became apparent to the teachers that these two groups, with different goals and aspirations and radically different skills, had much to offer each other. Thus the teachers created a heterogeneous science-technology course, team-taught by a math teacher, a science teacher, and a technology teacher.

During the year, the course curriculum is divided into three cycles: measurement, transportation, and communications. Students spend time with each teacher in each cycle. At the end of the year, all students have a goal to accomplish, which may be completed individually or in a small group. The year I visited, the assignment was to make something that would fly a certain distance, stay in the air a certain amount of time, and hit a target. The course always seeks to combine theory and application for real-life problems.

As might be expected, the Kennebunk faculty is divided in its views of the program's success. Clearly, learning that is problem-oriented teaches students much about real-life issues. Some faculty members believe that great strides are being made to create a true learning community in this classroom. Others fear that the course is too easy for the college-bound students and a waste of time, since it does not prepare them specifically for more advanced science classes. The verdict is not yet in, but everyone is watching the progress of the course.

Ninth-grade students who do not take the science-technology course enroll in Kennebunk's other ninth-grade science offering: oceanography. This class is specifically geared to Kennebunk's location on the southern coast of Maine. It was created to precede the traditional biology class. Oceanography teaches specific skills needed for biology, chemistry, and physics, while making use of local natural resources. In the fall, students learn about the characteristics of the local waters. They progress to historical geology, rock and mineral identification, and the study of the organisms found in the sea near Maine. Their own community provides a wealth of information for the laboratory, and the course brings them in closer touch with the community.

Another class combining several disciplines was designed by the students themselves. Nine at-risk students asked the teachers to help them fashion a course that would be entirely problem-centered. They wanted to design and build a helicopter-like vehicle and believed they would need a variety of skills to do so. The course, three periods long, combines English, math, and science or technology; and the vehicle itself is now under construction. English skills are necessary, as the students read articles about aircraft, send letters of inquiry about materials, and publish their own newsletter. They have found math skills essential in order to measure accurately. Physics is needed to understand about flight. And technology is central to the entire course.

Of course, there are many frustrations. Sometimes the students have to wait for parts or materials, because they depend on donations and low prices. When a project goes on for too long, their interest wanes. Perhaps they need several projects going at once, but there are too few students to manage multiple projects. In spite of these difficulties, going to school now has become both exciting and relevant to these youngsters. One student told me, "We used to be problem-makers — now we're problem-solvers."

The Arts

Not all Kennebunk programs are caught up in faculty controversy. For example, the arts are supported by the school, the community, and a local non-profit foundation, River Tree Arts. There are four levels of art courses at the high school; and after the first year, students are encouraged to identify and follow their own areas of interest. Students write goals for their projects, identify a specific area of interest, research an artist who works in that area, locate samples of the artist's work, create and carry out their own work, and bring it to the class for discussion and critique. The process is lengthy and complex, but a timeline helps the students to maintain their focus.

An apprenticeship program permits talented students who progress beyond the school's offerings to continue to grow by working with a mentor out of school. These students are placed with local artists, and the school uses a grant to help pay the artists for their time. There are apprenticeships in jewelry making, ceramics, dance, music, and theater. The one requirement for all apprenticeships is that the students "pay back" the 40 hours of their apprenticeship by serving the school in some way, perhaps by teaching a skill they have learned, performing, or creating a school display.

At the end of the year, the mentors are invited to the school for a luncheon, which includes student performances and displays. River Tree Arts also funds many artists-in-residence. During a visit to the United States, an African dancer spent a week at Kennebunk High School, giving student workshops in the day, adult classes at night, and a dance performance at the end of the week. The public performance included participation by members of the workshops and classes. River Tree Arts also gives students scholarships for music lessons, sponsors poetry luncheons, and even organizes an adult and student chorale.

Kennebunk offers a rich performing arts curriculum. There are two dance classes, two theater classes, and many musical groups: a chorus, a concert band, a marching band, a wind ensemble, and three jazz bands — all with a student population of only 660! The concert band numbers 108 members, who practice in small groups at various times during the day; complex scheduling prevents the entire band from practicing together more than once before each concert. The marching band does not compete. Bruce Lewis, chairman of the music department, notes: "In competition we sometimes look for what the judges want instead of expressing ourselves. I want the students to understand what the composer was looking for and learn to communicate it. We're here to learn, not to impress people."

Other Special Opportunities

Most schools use computer labs, but few do so as effectively as the business department at Kennebunk High School. The teachers individualize instruction. They believe that since each student learns at a different pace at a computer, students with very different needs can be working together. One day a small office-procedures class will be using the dictaphone and practicing Word Perfect, while an English teacher and some students learn about desktop publishing. And a small class in computer programming will be working with their teacher as other students work independently. The room is busy, but not impossibly noisy. When I visited the school a month and a half before the end of the school year, the computer lab had already been used more than 17,900 times by individual students.

Another opportunity for students is service learning. Under the leadership of Headmaster McConnell, Kennebunk High School has joined the schools that mandate community service as a graduation requirement. The program was initiated two years ago, and each student must give 30 hours of service to non-profit organizations. A list of possible placements is posted in the guidance office, but the students initiate the contacts for their own placements. They volunteer at nursing homes and hospitals, babysit for the PTA, assist in elementary schools, and work with the police and parks and recreation departments. After students have completed their hours, they check in at the guidance office and a counselor verifies their participation.

There are also opportunities to get an early start on college. The University of New England, a liberal arts college with a strong program in osteopathy and many science courses, is not far from Kennebunk High School. Any Kennebunk senior may take one tuition-free course per semester at the university and receive both high school and college credit. And any senior who has almost completed high school and would like to study at the university may enroll there full-time at a greatly reduced tuition. They are still eligible to be involved in high school sports and social events while taking college-level courses. For students interested in biological sciences, this has been an especially rewarding experience.

Teacher Accreditation

Teacher accreditation in Maine is different than in most states, and Kennebunk's own system goes beyond that of the rest of the state. Beginning teachers in Maine, no matter how strong their background, are issued two-year provisional certificates. When they are hired, they have a support team to mentor them and evaluate their progress. At the end of two years, with the team's approval, they receive a professional certificate. If the team believes that the new teacher is not ready to be professionally certified, the provisional certificate may be extended for another year. At the end of that time, the new teacher either becomes certified or must leave the profession. The professional certificate must be renewed every five years, and the teacher must have completed at least six credits relating to his or her teaching area to be eligible for renewal. Three years after receiving a professional certificate, teachers may apply to become a master teacher, which confers no extra salary.

In Kennebunk, master teachers may apply for two further professional levels. The application procedure includes a self-evaluation and portfolio and an evaluation by a panel. The community rewards these advanced professionals with higher salaries. The highest extra salary for each teacher at this top professional level is $7,000 above the standard pay scale. The money shows teachers that the community cares about their contributions and gives them a special status that is missing in standardized salary schedules, reinforcing the closeness of Kennebunk's school and its community.

Conclusion

I have attempted to give readers a glimpse of 12 schools that succeed. How many more schools might succeed if they did not face the uphill battles for essential educational funds? A familiar poster hangs in many schools, suggesting that society would be different if schools received all the money they needed while the Air Force had to run a bake sale in order to build a new bomber. That's something to consider. We may throw billions of dollars into a Star Wars program without any sure sign that these dollars will be spent usefully or any certainty that our society will have the resources to see the program to completion. When we do increase school expenditures, we expect SAT scores to soar immediately and American high school students to begin leading the world in math and science virtually overnight. We do not give them enough time, enough money, or any benefit of the doubt. It must be done perfectly, today. Nowhere else in our society do we hold such unreasonable expectations.

One reason that our students are performing less well is that their families are performing less well. We, as a society, have not been as successful in assisting families to become a strong support system as we were in times past. Instead, we expect our schools to step into the breach. We expect education to cure the ills of our culture and our time.

Nevertheless, in the absence of ideal conditions and in our imperfect society, many schools are proof that the entire system need not be changed in order to make vast improvements in individual schools. It is too easy merely to wait for the revolution that will create a wondrous new educational system. It is harder to look at existing schools and improve them in small but significant ways. But that is exactly what the hard-working administrators, teachers, parents, and students in the Blue Ribbon schools do.

The 12 Blue Ribbon schools that I have profiled in this book can be helpful on two levels. First, they are exemplars of specific programs that can be broadly adapted. The examples are numerous: Banneker's community service program that requires students to reach out to others; New Trier's advisory program, providing teenagers with a daily time and place to deal with problems and concerns; Craftsbury's school trips, uniting faculty and students in an out-of-school learning experience; St. Johnsbury's vocational programs, preparing graduates for jobs in their own town; South Brunswick's CIPED Program, giving students a mentor while they sample careers. These programs were developed in response to perceived needs in their communities. Many communities have similar needs and could adapt all or many aspects of these programs.

Second, there are significant educational concepts identifiable in most of these schools that can have an impact on any school. Every school can be improved by giving new support systems to students who are in trouble and to new teachers. A mentor for each new teacher can be a crucial factor in their success. A faculty or peer mentor for each student who is experiencing difficulty can change the entire school environment by cutting into undercurrents of anger and anti-intellectualism.

The programs that take students out of school and into the community to volunteer, to learn about a career, or to study may cost no more than minimal transportation fees. They can be established anywhere, and they have proven to generate powerful results. Sometimes students find their vocational direction. Sometimes they are able to help someone in need. Their intellectual growth can be significant. One result is inevitable: The community is brought together through the new relationships between the generations. It becomes a kinder place to live, in which people of different ages come to know and trust each other. As I viewed these programs in action, I was astonished to see how many adults enjoy being a mentor for a teenager and how many teenagers blossom as role models for younger children or as a support for the aged. There is abundant anecdotal evidence suggesting that all of us, especially young people, respond positively to interest and encouragement with an increased will to succeed.

Any school can grow when faculty, students, administrators, and parents sit down together, discuss the future, and hammer out realistic goals for the school.

All 12 of these schools have learned to use their local resources, which vary widely. Every community has businesses or individuals who want to contribute to a local foundation, which can support grants in the arts, for innovative teaching practices, or for a piece of equipment the school badly needs. Other local resources can include hospitals, theaters, zoos, museums, and universities; these resources offer lecturers, partnerships, and challenging learning experiences for students.

94

Unlike many businesses, most school systems cannot afford a full-time person to measure the success of new programs. Teachers, already stretched to their limits and giving up free time to improve the way that they work with students, are satisfied if they see growth and achievement. They should collect data, but that is the task that overworked people often let go. Nevertheless, the anecdotal data provided in these pages lends much encouragement and food for thought.

These are schools that are taking giant steps. In our imperfect world, we can learn from them.